Drafting Legislation for Sustainable Soils: A Guide

Ian Hannam and Ben Boer

IUCN Environmental Law Programme

IUCN Environmental Policy and Law Paper No. 52

IUCN – The World Conservation Union
2004

The designation of geographical entities in this book, and the presentation of the material, do not imply the expression of any opinion whatsoever on the part of IUCN concerning the legal status of any country, territory, or area, or of its authorities, or concerning the delimitation of its frontiers or boundaries.

The views expressed in this publication do not necessarily reflect those of IUCN, IWMI or BMZ.

This publication has been made possible in part by funding from IWMI and BMZ.

Published by: IUCN, Gland, Switzerland and Cambridge, UK

IUCN
The World Conservation Union

IWMI
International Water Management Institute

Citation: Hannam, Ian and Boer, Ben (2004). *Drafting Legislation for Sustainable Soils: A Guide*. IUCN, Gland, Switzerland and Cambridge, UK. x + 100 pp.

ISBN: 2-8317-0813-3

Cover design by: IUCN Publications Services Unit

Front cover photo: Soil degradation and reclamation at Kjolur, Iceland, *Dr Andres Arnalds, Soil Conservation Institute, Iceland.*

Back cover photo: Sustainable soil landscape, Attunga, NSW, Australia, *Richard McEvoy, Newport, Australia*

Layout by: Bookcraft Ltd, Stroud, UK

Produced by: IUCN Publications Services Unit

Printed by: Page Bros, Norwich, UK

Available from: IUCN Publications Services Unit
219c Huntingdon Road, Cambridge CB3 ODL, United Kingdom
Tel: +44 1223 277894, Fax: +44 1223 277175
E-mail: info@books.iucn.org
www.iucn.org/bookstore
A catalogue of IUCN publications is also available

The text of this book is printed on Fineblade Extra 90gsm made from low chlorine pulp

Drafting Legislation for Sustainable Soils: A Guide

Table of contents

Preface

We are pleased to jointly present this important new publication of the IUCN Environmental Law Programme (ELP), on drafting legislation for sustainable soils.

The World Summit on Sustainable Development recognised the importance of promoting programmes for the environmentally sound, effective and efficient use of soil fertility. This Guide, intended to primarily serve as a resource for States to assist their endeavours to reform legislation and institutions to protect and manage soils, will contribute to that aim.

There are many reasons that may trigger the development and adoption of a sound legal and institutional framework for sustainable soils, such as the necessity to create an enabling environment for farmers and agencies to adopt sound management practices to enhance productivity levels of water and land.

A sound legal and institutional framework for managing soils is not only critical for food production, but also for biological diversity conservation and poverty alleviation. This Guide addresses all these aspects. One of the most striking features of this publication is that it proposes legal and institutional elements that specifically address the needs of disadvantaged people, particularly women. This is unique, as there are not many examples of legal frameworks relating to natural resource management that specifically seek to accommodate the concerns of the poor. This Guide also highlights the need for national soil policy and sets out the elements of a soil management plan.

From the International Water Management Institute (IWMI) perspective, the publication is an extension of an IWMI sponsored study carried out by the one of the authors, Dr Ian Hannam, related to the legal and institutional aspects of land and water management in four Asian countries, namely, Bangladesh, China, Lao PDR, and the Philippines.

For IUCN, the Guide is the response to Resolution 2.59 from the 2nd World Conservation Congress, Amman 2000, which welcomed the initiative of the ELP to create a specialist group addressing the sustainable use of soils "to prepare guidelines and explanatory material relating to principles and elements of national legislation and policy to assist States to manage their specific soil degradation and land degradation problems".

This Guide for drafting soil legislation is very timely, bearing in mind the rapid rate at which soils are being degraded. It will be of enormous benefit to anyone who is seeking to advance the sustainable management of soils, and in particular States. In doing so, this work is making a valuable contribution to sustainable development, poverty alleviation, and to achieving the Millennium Development Goals.

Achim Steiner
IUCN Director General

Frank Rijsberman
IWMI Director General

Foreword

The IUCN Environmental Law Programme (ELP) welcomes this publication, a new product of the IUCN Commission on Environmental Law (CEL) Sustainable Soils Specialist Group.

In October 2000, the World Conservation Congress adopted Resolution 2.59, which called upon the ELP, in its development of legal guidelines and explanatory materials, to "pay particular attention to the ecological needs of soil and their ecological functions for the conservation of biological diversity and the maintenance of human life".

Less than a year later, the UNEP Montevideo III Programme, adopted by the UNEP Governing Council in 2001, included as one of its objectives the need "to improve the conservation, rehabilitation and sustainable use of soils".

In 2002, the ELP published the CEL Sustainable Soils Specialist Group's report entitled *Legal and Institutional Frameworks for Sustainable Soils* (EPLP No. 45), which analysed the treatment of soil-related issues in both national and international environmental law, and drew conclusions on needs at both levels.

This new publication complements the previous one and goes a step further in analysing all of the necessary features of a legal and institutional framework for the sustainable management and conservation of soils. It also provides guidance for the drafting of legislation.

Once again, this publication demonstrates in a very tangible way how members of the CEL volunteer network, now comprising over 975 environmental law specialists from 130 countries, contribute towards meeting the IUCN ELP mission of:

"laying the strongest possible legal foundation at the international, regional and national levels for environmental conservation in the context of sustainable development".

This book makes a most valuable contribution towards meeting this challenge. It serves to raise awareness and to help countries develop new, or update existing, legal and institutional frameworks that can contribute to sustainable and healthy soils and thereby help meet the challenge of the Millennium Development Goals.

The ELP is proud to be associated with the International Water Management Institute (IWMI) in the publication of this book, and is most grateful to the German Federal Ministry for Economic Cooperation and Development (BMZ) and to IWMI for funding the publication.

John Scanlon
Head, IUCN Environmental Law Programme
Director, IUCN Environmental Law Centre

Acknowledgements

This Guide is the second report of the Sustainable Soils Project of the IUCN Environment Law Programme (ELP). It is a further step in implementing the Soil Resolution of the 2000 Amman IUCN World Conservation Congress. The first report entitled *Legal and Institutional Frameworks for Sustainable Soils* (IUCN Environmental Policy and Law Paper No 45) was published in December 2002. Like the first report, this publication is the outcome of the continuing effective partnership between the fields of environmental law and soil science, specifically the ELP and a number of the key global soil science institutions, including: the International Union of Soil Sciences (IUSS); the World Association of Soil and Water Conservation (WASWC); the European Soil Bureau (European Commission) (ESB); Torba, Soils and Society (Montpellier, France); the International Soil Reference and Information Centre (Wageningen, The Netherlands) (ISRIC); and the International Water Management Institute (IWMI).

We wish to acknowledge the assistance of a number of people in the preparation of this second report. First, thanks go to Professor Nicholas Robinson, Chair of the Commission on Environmental Law, in establishing the sustainable use of soils project and his continuing encouragement for the Specialist Group Sustainable Soils (SGSS). Particular thanks go to John Scanlon, Head of the IUCN Environmental Law Programme (ELP) for his substantial interest in this Guide and his support in enabling a three-month secondment of Ian Hannam to the IUCN Environmental Law Centre (ELC) to undertake initial research to prepare the Guide. A special thanks also go to Dr Françoise Burhenne-Guilmin, Senior Counsel to the ELC, for her continuing support and assistance.

The continuing work of ELC Senior Legal Officer Dr Alejandro Iza as the ELC focal point for the project is gratefully acknowledged. The editorial comments and general comments on the direction of the report by the members of the CEL SGSS, Professor Antonio Herman Benjamin, Ketill Sigurjonsson, Lyle Glowka and Bill Futrell, were gratefully received.

Further, we are thankful for the work of Anni Lukács and Alexandra Fante of the ELC in assisting with background research and database materials and to Ann DeVoy for her role in publication services. We also acknowledge the constructive critique and encouraging comments from the soil science specialists of the expert reference group to the SGSS, including Professor Winfried Blum (Vienna, Austria), Dr Luca Montanarella (European Soils Bureau), Mr Sjef Kaufman, International Soil Reference and Information Centre (ISRIC), Dr Frits Penning deVries (IWMI), Professor Hans Hurni (IUSS), Professor Rabah Lahmar (Torba, Soil and Society) and Dr Martin Held (representing Torba, Soil and Society). Special mention should also be made of Dr Samran Sombatpanit (President WASWC) and Dr Roel Oldeman (former Director, ISRIC) for their institutional support. Our thanks also go to the Faculty of Law, University of Sydney, in providing study leave and infrastructure assistance for Ben Boer during the project. We acknowledge Dr Robert Smith, formerly Director-General of the former Department of Land and Water Conservation, NSW, Australia, and the infrastructure assistance of the new Department of Infrastructure, Planning and Natural Resources in the preparation of this Guide. Finally, we acknowledge each other, in working together closely and in harmony, melding the perspectives of two different but related disciplines, to put together a document that will hopefully be accessible to and used by a very wide range of professionals working in this vital field.

Dr Ian Hannam and Professor Ben Boer
Specialist Group Sustainable Soils, IUCN Commission on Environmental Law

Note from the authors

This Guide is intended to be used as a resource document for States to draw on to reform existing legislation to protect and manage soil, to establish the direction for the drafting of new national legislation for the sustainable use of soil, and to assist in the establishment or reform of associated institutions to manage and protect the ecological integrity of soil. The Guide has been prepared in response to Recommendation 7.4 of the IUCN Environmental Law Programme publication – *Legal and Institutional Frameworks for Sustainable Soils* ("The Report").[1]

Recommendation 7.4 reads:

"It is recommended that work continue on the development of the elements for a 'generic' national soil statute, but to expand this task to include the development of legal frameworks and/or regional instruments for particular regions of the world".

The Report has had a significant bearing on the choice, and format of the legislative elements suggested in this Guide. Users of the Guide are advised to refer to the Report for further background to the concepts and the legal and institutional factors that were used to arrive at its Recommendations.

---

1 See Hannam, I.D. with B.W. Boer, 2002, *Legal and Institutional Frameworks for Sustainable Soils: A Preliminary Report*, Environmental Policy and Law Paper No. 45, IUCN, Gland, Switzerland and Cambridge, UK, and Bonn, Germany, Section 4, www.iucn.org/themes/law/pdfdocuments/EPLP45EN.pdf

I. Introduction

1. Introduction

Soil is the basis of virtually all terrestrial life. It is both an inherent part of biological diversity as well as the major part of its foundation. Without soil, human and many other forms of life on earth could not exist. It is with this understanding that this guide to drafting soil legislation is put forward. Its ethical underpinning is that we, as humans, have a responsibility to ensure that all life forms dependent on soil have an optimum right to a continued existence, in the short term as individuals and populations and in the longer term as species and ecosystems.

It has been forecast that the global human population will increase from the present 6 billion up to 8 billion by the year 2020.[2] In order that sufficient food will be provided, both for these additional people and to raise the standard of provision for those at present with an inadequate diet, a large increase in food production must take place. This increase in food production must come from approximately the same land area as is at present under agriculture, as the remainder is too dry, too wet, too cold, or too steep and mountainous to make a significant contribution. This inevitably means greater pressure will be put on prime lands, and especially those with the most fertile soils, to provide the extra food required. As demand increases, there will be increasing pressure also on the less productive soils, where the impact of soil degradation is most dramatically seen, even resulting in the displacement of people from their homelands.[3]

The effects of the increase in the human population on the world, especially in terms of the decline in food security, indicates that soil has ecological limits which change according to the variations within different ecosystems and the cultural relationships with the land and soil resources.[4] In this context, it is relevant to highlight the role that the element "water" plays in enabling the "soil" to be used within its inherent ecological capabilities and ecological limits to produce food and to supply other resources and raw materials for human needs. In some circumstances, the success of soil rehabilitation programs is dependent upon the ability of humans to effectively control and manage surface water and groundwater.[5] There is an

---

2 Population Division of the Department of Economic and Social Affairs of the United Nations Secretariat, *World Population Prospects: The 2002 Revision* and *World Urbanization Prospects*; the predictions differ slightly according to the variants used; http://esa.un.org/unpp/p2k0data.asp

3 From Bridges, E.M., I.D. Hannam, L.R. Oldeman, F. Penning deVries, S.J. Scherr, and S. Sombatpanit, 2002, (Eds.), *Response to Land Degradation*, Science Publishers, Inc, Enfield, (N.H), USA, p. 1; Hurni, H. and K. Meyer (Eds.), 2002, *A World Soils Agenda, Discussing International Actions for the Sustainable Use of Soils,* prepared with the support of an international group of specialists of the IASUS Working Group of the International Union of Soil Sciences (IUSS), Centre for Development and Environment, Berne.

4 See Penning deVries, F., H. Acquay, D. Molden, S.J. Scherr, C. Valentin, and O. Cofie, 2002, *Integrated land and water management for food and environmental security*. Comprehensive Assessment Research Paper 1, Colombo, Sri Lanka: Comprehensive Assessment Secretariat; M.A. Stocking, 2003, "Tropical Soils and Food Security: The Next 50 Years", *Science*, 302: 1356–1359; Lahmar, R., Held, M., and L. Montanarella, 2003, *People Matter: Food Security and Soils*, Torba Soil and Society / Soils and Societies, Montpellier.

5 There are many instances where countries have preferred to cater for "soil" and "water" issues in a

increasing imbalance in the production of food due to the difference in the rate of deterioration of soils and their functions and the rate of their regeneration. This situation requires an in-depth reconsideration of human attitudes to natural resources in general, but to soil in particular. This challenge has been taken up by the international soil science community,[6] which is attempting to create an awareness and knowledge of the sustainable use of soil among all humans. The main objectives of this movement are to:

- Change the attitude of humans about the vital importance of soils.
- Remind humans that soil is the foundation of human physical development and has a fundamental role in sustaining societies.
- Raise the "status" of soil by advising governments of the world of the way to manage their soil as a non-renewable resource.
- Build an international network of specialists to impede the progress of soil deterioration.

However, to successfully achieve these objectives, national and international frameworks for soil legislation need to be based on a clear understanding of the confusing differences in the use of terminology in the soil science, sociological, and ecological disciplines. A range of concepts and terms used to analyse the issues and risks associated with soil degradation has evolved, and these are not always used in the same way or consistently by the scientists in the relevant disciplines, let alone by different jurisdictions.

1.1 Soil and soil degradation

Soil

The processes involved in soil formation are complex[7] and definitions of soil reflect this complexity. The Council of Europe defines soil as:

> … an integral part of the earth's ecosystems and is situated at the interface between the earth's surface and bedrock. It is subdivided into successive horizontal layers with specific physical, chemical and biological characteristics. From the standpoint of history of soil use, and from an ecological and environmental point of view, the concept of soil also embraces porous sedimentary rocks and other permeable materials together with the water that these contain, and the reserves of underground water.[8]

This definition indicates that soil has a fundamental role in the terrestrial ecosystem as a three-dimensional body performing a wide range of functions, principally being ecological,

combined "soil and water conservation" law. However, the legislative elements for water in that type of legislation are primarily aimed at the farm-level of conservation and usage as against larger scale water allocation and impounding purposes.

6 Hurni and Meyer, 2002.

7 See Aswathanarayana, U., 1999, *Soil Resources and the Environment*, Science Publishers, Inc, Enfield, NH 03748, USA; Charman, P.E.V., and B.W. Murphy, (Eds.), 2000, *Soils: Their Properties and Management*, Oxford University Press, Melbourne; Gobat, J.M, M. Aragno and W. Matthey, 2003, *The Living Soil, Fundamentals of Soil Science and Soil Biology*, Science Publishers, Inc, Enfield, NH 03748, USA.

8 Council of Europe, *European Conservation Strategy – Recommendations for the 6th European Ministerial Conference on the Environment* (Council of Europe, 1990).

cultural, and land-use functions.[9] Any alteration of soil processes can lead to changes in the function of ecosystems. It must therefore be realised that many environmental problems, which become apparent in flora and fauna may originate from changes in the soil on which the flora and fauna is dependent. This same principle is also particularly important in the case of soil-water relationships. The amount of water contained in soil, or in transit by drainage through the soil, is critical for soil fertility, soil-plant relationships etc, whereas the amount of water that directly falls on, or flows over the soil surface can determine the amount and severity of soil erosion. This latter situation is also important for water conservation. It is essential that the principal functions of soil must strongly influence the preparation of legal frameworks for soil. The ecological functions, in particular, should be qualitatively and quantitatively safeguarded and preserved in the long term to ensure conservation of biodiversity in general and the maintenance of human life in particular. The functions of soil have been incorporated within at least one international convention[10] and many pieces of domestic legislation refer to various individual soil functions.[11]

Soil degradation

Soil degradation is broadly defined as a loss or reduction of soil functions or soil uses,[12] thus lowering the potential capability of the soil to produce ecosystem services. It includes physical, chemical, and biological deterioration, including loss of organic matter, decline in soil fertility, decline in structural condition, erosion, adverse changes in salinity, acidity or alkalinity, and the effects of toxic chemicals, pollutants or excessive flooding.[13]

Six specific processes are recognised as the main contributors to soil degradation: water erosion, wind erosion, waterlogging and excess salts, chemical degradation, physical degradation, and biological degradation.

Soil degradation now affects one-third of the world's soils that are used for agriculture, particularly the soils that are physically and chemically unsuitable for agriculture, grazing, and other purposes. The dominant process is erosion by wind and water, accounting for 83% of the area affected by soil degradation in the world. It has been demonstrated that land use systems are affected in all eco-regions and in most countries, although the impacts differ depending on the type, the severity and extent of soil degradation. The most important factors that contribute to a

---

9 See Sheals, J.G., Ed., 1969, *The Soil Ecosystem*: Systematic Aspects of the Environment, Organisms and Communities, The Systematics Association, Publication No. 8, Staples Printers Ltd, London.

10 See *Protocol on the Implementation of the Convention concerning the Protection of the Alps of 1991 in the area of Soil Protection* (Salzburg, 1991), Article 1, found at: http://fletcher.tufts.edu/multi/texts/bh993a.txt, but not yet in force. Article 1 sets out the multifunctional role of soil in an effective manner. See also The Soil Campaign, *Save Our Soil to Sustain Our Society, Appendix p. 34, Sheet One,* "The Functions Fulfilled by Soil" (in summary): According to current knowledge, soils are biomass production systems; substance transformation systems; regulation systems; a gene reserve; a memory. They are a page in the history of nature and of human evolution: Physical supports for all human activities (agriculture, industry, transport, habitat, craftwork, leisure etc): www.alliance21.org/en/proposals/finals/final_sols_en.rtf: See also the draft revised European Soil Charter of 2002 (found at www.nature.coe.int/CO-DBP6/codbp02e_02.doc), which includes an explicit description of the functions of soil.

11 See Hannam with Boer, 2002, Section 4, sub-section 2.3.

12 P.E.V., Charman and B.W. Murphy, Eds., 2000, *Soils: Their Properties and Management*, Oxford University Press, South Melbourne, Australia, see chapters 2, 3 and 4.

13 *Supra.*

state of soil degradation, and thus must be taken in account within a legal framework, include:

The intrinsic factors of soil degradation. These are the influences of climate, terrain, vegetation and biodiversity, especially the characteristics of soil biodiversity. However, the actual causes of soil degradation are the agents that determine the rate of degradation. These are:

- Biophysical: land use and land management, including deforestation and tillage methods;
- Socio-economic: human population, land tenure, marketing, institutions, income and human health; and
- Political forces: (pressure of incentives, political ideology, etc), that influence the processes of soil degradation.

The biophysical land characteristics. The natural resistance of soil to the forces of degradation depends on the inherent characteristics of soil (physical and chemical attributes) and the climatic conditions (mainly the amount and intensity of rainfall). Soils can range from highly resistant or stable to extremely sensitive and fragile. Stable soils may be in a steady-state condition at a particular point in time due to the effectiveness of an appropriate system of land use, whereas fragile soils can progressively degrade to a new steady-state when subjected to stress.

The relative area of degraded soil as a percentage of the total area of an individual country varies considerably around the world. There can be one or more causes for each type of soil degradation process, for example:

- *Agricultural activities:* the improper management of cultivated arable soils including insufficient or excessive use of fertilisers, shortening of the fallow period in shifting cultivation, use of poor quality irrigation water, absence or inadequate maintenance of erosion control measures, untimely or too frequent use of heavy machinery, water or wind erosion, compaction, loss of nutrients, salinisation, and soil pollution (by pesticides and fertilisers).
- *Removal of natural vegetation:* the excessive clearing of natural vegetation is one of the world's major environmental concerns. Deforestation of primary or secondary forest to convert the forest into agricultural land, palm oil plantations, large-scale commercial forestry, road construction and urban development cause soil erosion and loss of nutrients. Natural grasslands have been extensively cleared for arable agriculture, paving the way for extensive water and wind erosion.
- *Over-exploitation of vegetation for domestic use:* this activity does not necessarily involve the complete removal of the naturally occurring vegetation, but rather a degeneration of the remaining vegetation thus offering insufficient protection against soil erosion. It includes activities such as excessive gathering of fuel-wood, fodder and unsustainable timber extraction.
- *Overgrazing:* overgrazing by livestock leads to loss of vegetation cover, but also causes soil compaction by livestock trampling. Overgrazing predisposes soil to water and wind erosion.
- *Industrial activities:* includes all human activities of an industrial nature: industries, power generation, infrastructure and urbanisation, waste handling, traffic, etc. It is most often linked to soil pollution of different kinds (either point source or diffuse) and loss of soil productivity.

1.2 What is wrong with the national legislation in many jurisdictions?

An overview of current national legislation directed to soil indicates that States have adopted a wide variety of legislative approaches to deal with specific soil protection and management problems. This is generally reflected in the broad structural features of soil legislation, as well as in the variety of specific mechanisms used to protect and manage soil and land use.[14] The following observations can be made with regard to legislative systems relating to soil:

- States have been reasonably creative and innovative in the choice and application of individual mechanisms.
- Some States have developed a framework of legislation to manage a number of distinct soil and land use problems but generally lack linking or coordinating mechanisms to ensure that there is an effective institutional implementation of the legislation.
- The majority of legislation does not take into account the inherent ecological characteristics and limitations of soil bodies as the premise for land use decision-making; rather, the legislation related to soil addresses soil problems ex post facto; i.e. to try to rectify the problems caused by poor land use planning or inappropriate land use in the first place.
- The legislation does not acknowledge soil as an ecological element with a central role in terrestrial ecology, the conservation of biodiversity and maintenance of environmental amenity.
- The primary functions of soil are not well represented in the legislation in most jurisdictions and only a few laws refer to the ecological features or needs of the soil.
- A dominant characteristic of existing national soil legislation is that it is directed to the physical problems caused by inappropriate land use, mainly agriculture and forestry (reflecting short-term private interests as against long-term public interest).
- Following from the last point, the structure of some laws indicates that they are a reaction to a political or institutional issue, rather than being designed to effectively manage the soil.
- Many individual laws do not have a clear statement of purpose or objectives. Where the intention is clear, it is often poorly reflected in the substance of the legislation.
- Many laws do not include the range of elements necessary to effectively protect or manage the particular soil problem, and where they do, those elements are often not logically developed. There are also many examples where the exact meaning or intention of the element is not apparent.
- There is generally a lack of consistency in the use of standard scientific soil terminology, and often there is an absence of definitions, or inadequate and poorly stated definitions.

14 For a comprehensive review and discussion of national soil legislation see Hannam with Boer, 2002, p. 40–41; Boer, B.W, and I.D. Hannam, 2003, Legal Aspects of Sustainable Soils; International and National, *Review of European Community and International Environmental Law*, 12:2, 149.

2. Use of this guide

Users of this Guide should refer to the IUCN Environmental Law Programme publication – *Legal and Institutional Frameworks for Sustainable Soils* ("The Report")[15] – for a more comprehensive analysis of the legal and institutional factors that have been used as a basis for the statements and recommendations found in Sections II to V below.

2.1 What is "soil legislation"?

Individual States have adopted a variety of approaches to frame domestic soil legislation, which were summarised in the Report in eight categories. The categories reflect the principal intent of the legislation; e.g., control of "soil erosion", control of "soil pollution", prevention of "soil degradation", "establishment of soil conservation institutions or an authority," etc.[16]

Comprehensive procedures for soil protection and management can, of course, be integrated into broader legislation that sets out responsibilities for the protection and management of other aspects of the environment (e.g. forests, water, biodiversity, desertification, land management, land administration).[17]

This Guide is thus intended to be used according to the specific legislative needs and priorities of a State for the protection and management of soil. It can be used as the basis for framing specialised legislation specifically addressing soil matters, or for assisting the process of integrating legislative elements for soil within an existing environmental law, or framing a new broad environmental law.

2.2 Legal and institutional elements

In this Guide, a legal and institutional "element" is a basic, essential component of a legal and institutional system.[18] An element can be a principle, a rule of conduct or a power to achieve a

---

15 Hannam, I.D. with B.W. Boer, 2002.

16 Hannam, I.D. with B.W. Boer, 2002, pp. 36–40.

17 In the practical sense, the types of legislation that may fall within the parameters of "soil legislation" (as used in the Guide) will often have a direct role and relationship with the management and use of agricultural land or "agrarian land". "Agrarian land" (as outlined in Introduction, p. xiii, to, Grossman, M.R, and W. Brussaard, *Agrarian Land Law in the Western World*, C.A.B International, Wallingford, UK), "forms an important component of the world's land surface, and in many nations, agricultural, forestry, and other rural uses occupy a majority of the area. The agrarian land provides the basic resource for cultivating the food and fibre products essential for humankind. But in addition, agrarian land is valued for its open space, for its contribution to the natural environment, and for its conservation, landscape, and aesthetic values".
Law that falls within the concept of "soil legislation" as presented in this Guide, plays an important role in the allocation and use of agrarian land and it is expected that there will be many instances where individual nations may consider the role and benefits of "soil legislation" in this context.

18 For a more comprehensive discussion on the concept of an "essential element" and its practical application, see Hannam, I.D., 2004, *A Method to Identify and Evaluate the Legal and Institutional Framework for the Management of Water and Land in Asia: The Outcome of a Study in Southeast Asia and the People's Republic of China,* Research Report 73. Colombo, Sri Lanka: International Water Management Institute.

particular legal purpose. An element can be used singly, or in combination with other elements, to promote actions for the achievement of the sustainable use of soil.[19] An individual law can include a number of elements in a format that gives an organization the power it needs, through its executive and administrative responsibilities, to achieve the sustainable use of soil.[20]

These elements may be distributed among a number of individual laws in a national legal and institutional system. The "essential elements" suggested in this Guide were developed through an evaluation of legal and ecological principles aimed at achieving a desired standard of performance in sustainable soil management.[21]

The legal and institutional elements suggested in this Guide can be used in several roles:

- To assist in assessing the capacity (defined below) of an existing instrument to meet prescribed standards of performance for the sustainable use of soil.[22] Depending on the assessed capacity of the law to achieve these standards, additional elements may be formulated.
- To guide the reform of an existing soil law, or to develop new legislation for the sustainable use of soil. Each legal and institutional element must have the capacity to achieve a prescribed level of ecological management or standard for soil.

The elements in the Guide generally fall within the following broad categories of legal and institutional elements to be found in a law or legal instrument:

General intent: Includes a clearly identifiable statement of the intended purpose of a legal instrument, which has a direct relationship to the general objective for the sustainable use of soils. It may be expressed either as a single or multi-functional statement, but may also be a series of independent statements that collectively convey the intent and purpose of the legal instrument.

Jurisdiction: Includes various statements or functions in a legal instrument that establish its interest over soil in a geographical and legal sense, including jurisdiction of a State, or of a specific organization, and which create a legal right to engage in some aspect of soil protection and management. It is often expressed as a sphere of authority and the territorial range of authority, and is synonymous with power, authority, or control.[23]

Responsibility. Includes the various functions that establish or enable a commitment to an objective

---

19 An essential element may also be referred to as a "legal concept" which is a term that has a specific meaning in a legal context: see Bodansky, D., 1995, "Customary (and not so Customary) International Environmental Law", *Indiana Journal of Global Legal Studies*, 3,1:105, who discusses the use of non-legal norms in international environmental law; many of these are also applicable to national laws; also, Chapter 5 "Environmental quality norms" in the *Environmental Code of Sweden, 1999*, see http://icm.noaa.gov/laws/Env_Code_1998_SE.pdf

20 See explanations of "Responsibility" and "Hierarchy of Responsibility" below.

21 Hannam, 2004.

22 "Law" in this context means a body of law enacted by a legislature, e.g., an act, decree, regulation, code, or other formal legal instrument that is legally enforceable. It can include agreements or covenants that are expressed to be legally binding.

23 It can also refer to "jurisdiction" exercised by a court, or system of courts in relation to the extent of legal authority conferred by the legislation.

of sustainable use of soil, and obligations, which establish a level of accountability to particular stated functions. There may be a division of responsibility in an instrument, and stated responsibilities may often directly express, create or invoke circumstances of "use rights" or "user rights".[24]

Goals and objectives: Includes a group of statements that express a policy position or strategic position in a legal instrument. Together they express a determination to engage in and to achieve the sustainable use of soil at a general, and/or technically specified level. The goals and objectives may be expressed in a single or multi-functional statement, but may comprise a number of multi-functional statements.

Definitions: Includes the presence of statements or terminology that defines or describe the meaning of key words, phrases or terms in a form that directly relate to the operation of the legal instrument. They may also convey intent to engage in a prescribed level of action, or achieve a particular standard for the sustainable use of soil. Definitions are used to interpret the legislation, in either a general sense of understanding, scope and application, or in a direct, technical operational sense relating to the role in the implementation of the law.

Duty of care: Includes the presence of terminology, functions, activities, policies and strategic materials that convey a legal and ethical commitment to take reasonable and practical steps to achieve sustainable use of soil. They may create a duty on the part of a person, a number of persons, a corporation or levels of administration, or a statutory entity, to comply with the law, in a prescribed manner, and can be in the form a general duty of care or a specific statutory duty of care.[25]

Hierarchy of responsibility: Includes the terminology and functions that create a responsibility and commitment to achieve sustainable use of soil through a number of different levels of administration, and with a variety of administrative functions. Through the structure of an organizational or institutional "hierarchy", particular "rights" and "obligations" may be established at respective levels of administration for individuals or for specific classes of people.

Institutional: Includes the presence of functions, statements, objectives and goals that give a particular organization or related administrative bodies, a direct responsibility for the sustainable use of soil. This usually occurs via a number of mechanisms including the policies and objectives of the organization, and the rules and regulations, incentive mechanisms,

---

24 This may be in the form of communal tenure, communal rights or individual property and use rights; Common property rights regimes include: access, communal property, private property, State property; property right regimes include both property rights (entitlements defining rights and duties in the use of natural resources), and property rules (the rules under which those rights and duties are exercised); see Oglethorpe, J., (Ed.), 1998, *Tenure and Sustainable Use,* SUI Technical Series Vol 2, IUCN, Gland, Switzerland; see also Burns, B.R. and R.S. Meinzen-Dick, (Eds.), 2000, *Negotiating Water Rights*, International Food Policy Research Institute, Vistaar Publications, New Delhi; Boelens, R. and P. Hoogendam (Eds.), 2002, *Water Rights and Empowerment*, Koninglijke Van Gorcum, The Netherlands.

25 A duty of care could require individuals who influence a risk of harm to the environment to take "reasonable and practical steps" to prevent such harm; a statutory duty of care could apply to harm that may be caused, both harm to living entities and harm to those yet to have life (this reflects the principle of intergenerational equity). A duty of care may also be subject to an express set of principles or rules laid out in the legislation; see Bates, G., 2001, *A Duty of Care for the Protection of Biodiversity on Land*, Report to the Productivity Commission, Commonwealth of Australia.

accountability mechanisms, norms, traditions, plans and procedures, practices and customs that govern its operations.[26]

Policy: Includes statements about an intended course of action, and may include statements of an attitudinal, principled or strategic nature, and/or the existence of any function or activity that enable the development of materials for these purposes, to achieve the sustainable use of soil. It also includes statements referring to the need for a review or reform of legislation, including a commitment to the preparation of particular types of legal instruments and the timing of such actions.[27]

Education: Includes functions, activities, policies or statements relating to educational activities aimed at achieving the sustainable use of soil. These would include technical training courses, skills development programs, the preparation and dissemination of materials for these activities.

Research and investigation: Includes functions, activities and programs that encourage or specify a commitment to a systematic investigation into activities that produce information and knowledge of a scientific, technical, sociological, economic or cultural nature aimed at the sustainable use of soil.

Community participation: Refers to the presence of functions, activities, and programs in a legal instrument that enable interaction with a community of people, to engage in the undertaking of various participatory activities relating to sustainable use of soil. It includes references to: general capacity-building, improving awareness, knowledge and skills, problem identification, or some form of technical or practical activity related to the sustainable use of soil. It may also include a mechanism for stakeholders to have formal communication with an organization on problem identification, problem-solving, decision-making and consultative processes aimed at the sustainable use of soil.[28]

Soil planning: Includes the presence of statements, functions, activities or programs in a legal instrument that enable a role in planning the sustainable use of soil. It includes references to technical surveys, data base development, assembling knowledge on the ecological distribution of soil, the ecological condition of soil, preparing standards for use of soil, natural resource evaluation, soil classification, environmental assessment, plan development, soil zoning, references to plan implementation, monitoring plans and actions, and the preparation of explanatory materials.

---

26 An "organization" is a positive entity designed by their creators to maximize wealth, income, or other objectives defined by the opportunities afforded by the institutional structure of the society; see North, D.C., 1990, *Institutions, institutional change and economic performance*, New York, Cambridge University Press; Bandaragoda, D. J., 2000, *A framework for institutional analysis for water resources management in a river basin context*, Working Paper 5, Colombo, Sri Lanka, International Water Management Institute; see Bridges *et al.*, 2002, Chapter 8 "Institutional Innovations".

27 Bridges *et al.*, 2002, Chapter 9 "Law and Policy" includes various examples and approaches to national soil policies.

28 See Article 19, *United Nations Convention to Combat Desertification in Countries Experiencing Serious Drought and/or Desertification, Particularly in Africa* (Paris, 17 June 1994); 33 ILM (1994), 1328.

Soil management: Includes the presence of statements, functions, activities and programs in a legal instrument that enable the preparation and direct implementation of soil conservation programs. It includes references to specific types of soil conservation works, projects and design criteria, the construction and implementation of the works and projects, and monitoring the outcome of implementation. This element also considers processes for the development of environmental standards, limits of use, including the criteria and matters of concern for their development, and specifies the implementation process.

Finance: Includes the presence of statements, functions, activities or programs in a legal instrument that provide for the financing of projects or activities, or raising money for the sustainable use of soil. It may include reference to budgetary procedures, specific appropriation funds and soil environment funds.

Implementation and enforcement: Includes the presence of statements, functions, or mechanisms in a legal instrument that must be observed, or complied with at a defined standard, or in the form of a direct obligation, or prescribed standard of behaviour. It is often referred to as a regulation, or a regulatory role. It may be through a legal notice or direction from a regulator or through a court order. It also includes the procedure to carry out this role, and to regulate certain activities that are directly beneficial to the sustainable use of soil. Enforcement functions may include responsibilities to identify particular types of offences, investigate certain matters, gather evidence, take direct remedial actions, confiscate certain items, and initiate prosecution. The legislation may also set out the range and limits of monetary penalty for specified offences and provision for appeal.

Dispute resolution: Includes the presence of statements, functions, activities or programs, in a legal instrument that enables the settlement of a conflict, or a disagreement between parties, generally over access to, or a perceived right of access to land or the use of land. Various processes and facilities are available for dispute resolution including conciliation processes, mediation processes, arbitration and the courts. These procedures normally include provisions for appeal.

2.3 Measuring the capacity of a legal and institutional framework to achieve the sustainable use of soil

This part of the Guide focuses on measuring the capacity of a legal and institutional framework to manage and prevent soil degradation to achieve the sustainable use of soil. The "capacity" is determined by the number and type of essential legal and institutional elements present within the relevant laws and legal instruments, in a format that enables the sustainable use of soil to be identified, and with the legal, administrative and technical capability within the particular instrument to take some form of positive action. In some cases, the capacity will be direct and obvious. In other places, it will exist in a format that enables some form of indirect action. Capacity is represented in the form of legal rights, the type of legal mechanisms, and importantly, the number and comprehensiveness of the essential elements identified above.[29]

[29] Boer and Hannam, 2003, p. 155.

Most key soil management issues are multi-factorial (i.e. many include a sociological, a legal and a technical component), so generally more than one piece of environmental legislation, along with detailed regulations, will be needed to effectively manage each individual soil degradation issue. A variety of types of legal and institutional elements and mechanisms may also be required. This reinforces the necessity to analyse the existing environmental legislation (if any) at each level in any jurisdiction in order to ascertain current management regimes and their interactions (if any). The information generated by such an analysis may also be used as a guide as to the type of legislative and institutional elements that may be necessary to include within any new legislative regime that may be drafted for each level of soil degradation control and management.[30]

2.4 A legal and institutional system

A legal and institutional system is the organizational and operational regime that is used to manage the sustainable use of soil. It is important, when a State is designing such a regime, that it reviews its current organizational system to ensure that it has the capability to effectively administer a new law. In some circumstances an organization (or several organizations) may have to be partly or wholly re-organized to effectively administer the legal and institutional responsibilities for the sustainable use of soil.[31]

2.5 Key principles for the sustainable use of soil

The two principal sources that established the direction for the development of the suggested elements in this Guide for drafting national soil legislation include:

- Ecological and scientific principles for the sustainable use of soil.
- The Resolution of the IUCN World Conservation Congress of 2000 on Sustainable Use of Soil.

2.5.1 Ecological principles for the sustainable use of soil

Some of the more important principles include:

- Soil degradation affects the global environment because it represents a loss of integral components of the world's ecosystems and global biodiversity.
- Accelerated soil degradation is mostly human-induced and occurs in all eco-regions of the world, irrespective of social, economic, and political conditions.
- A recognition that soil degradation has a significant impact on the total environment in any particular State.
- The extent, type, degree and severity of soil degradation vary between one soil community and another.

30 Boer and Hannam, 2003, p. 115.

31 Hannam with Boer, 2002, Section 4.

- Agricultural soils are being lost to non-agricultural uses, especially urbanization.
- Soil degradation causes damage to the soil resource by erosion, contamination, change of physical or chemical state (acidification, compaction, and salinisation) and loss of nutrients and organic matter.
- A significant proportion of the degradation of the atmosphere is due to greenhouse gas emissions caused by various forms of soil use associated with agriculture.[32]
- Loss of biodiversity is generally related to land use changes, including deforestation, agricultural intensification and urban expansion, which cause soil degradation.
- Accelerated soil degradation exacerbates the scarcity of productive lands and is a major threat to global food security and induces poverty.

The general characteristics of the current global situation with land resource use also give direction to the need for improved international and national soil legal and institutional frameworks, including:[33]

- The uneven spatial and temporal distribution among nations of populations and consumptive needs.
- The links that have been established between the occurrence of soil degradation and poverty.
- The uneven distribution of productive, unutilized, and under-utilized or degrading soils.
- The substantial variation in cropping systems, and occurrence of productive soils.
- Areas of surplus production and of food deficit.
- Availability of capital for soil protection is varied.
- The opportunities that exist to transfer knowledge on sustainable use of soils, combat degradation, and achieve sustainable land management vary between regions and nations.
- Consideration of the global soil environment should be independent of political boundaries.

2.5.2 The Resolution of the IUCN World Conservation Congress of 2000 on Sustainable Use of Soil

The Resolution of the IUCN World Conservation Congress of 2000 on Sustainable Use of Soil, requests the IUCN Environmental Law Programme, in its development of legal guidelines and explanatory material, and investigation into a global legal instrument for the sustainable use of soils, in particular to "pay particular attention to the ecological needs of soil and their ecological functions for the conservation of biodiversity and the maintenance of human life".[34] The Report

32 See Hannam, I.D., 2004, International and National Aspects of a Legislative Framework to Manage Soil Carbon Sequestration, *Climate Change, An Interdisciplinary, International Journal Devoted to the Description, Causes and Implications of Climatic Change.*

33 See Wood, S., K. Sebastion and S.J. Scherr, 2000, *Pilot Analysis of Global Ecosystems. Agroecosystems*. International Food Policy Research Institute and World Resources Institute, Washington D.C; Hurni and Meyer, 2003; Boer and Hannam, 2003.

indicates that this statement refers to the development of legal and institutional elements that will enable an ecosystem-based approach to be applied in all aspects of soil protection and management. As noted in the Report, "Such a process is likely to have a different outcome from a process that relies merely on the application of the conventional, scientific and objective principles of ecology to protect and manage soil. This is because the ecosystem approach studies the *relationship* between soils, as living ecological communities, and the environment. An effective legal system for the sustainable use of soil will therefore depend on the use of appropriate ecological concepts and development of a legal and institutional system with a capacity to implement these concepts."[35]

2.6 The Guide and other environmental strategies

It is intended that this Guide will assist in implementing some of the key objectives of various important global environmental strategies, including:

- The UNEP Montevideo Programme III 2000.
- The Plan of Implementation of the World Summit on Sustainable Development 2002.
- The World Soils Agenda 2002.
- The Committee for the Review of the Implementation of the Convention to Combat Desertification.
- UNEP's Strategy on Land Use Management and Soil Conservation.

2.6.1 UNEP Montevideo Programme III

The Montevideo Programme III – the Programme for the Development and Periodic Review of Environmental Law for the First Decade of the Twenty-First Century was finalised in 2001, and emphasises the implementation of environmental law.[36] The programme includes a specific Objective for Soils (Objective 12):

Objective:

To improve the conservation, rehabilitation and sustainable use of soils.

Strategy:

Promote the development and implementation of laws and policies for enhancing the conservation, sustainable use and, where appropriate, rehabilitation of soils.

Action:

(a) Review domestic land use laws, change of land use laws and tenure systems with the aim of achieving soil conservation and reclamation goals;

---

34 See Hannam with Boer, 2002, Section 1, for complete wording of the Amman Resolution on Sustainable Use of Soil.

35 *Supra*, p. 17.

36 *Decision 21/33 of the 2001 Governing Council of UNEP*, February 2001 (www.unep.org/GC/GC21/Documents/gc-21-INF-03/K0000295.E.pdf).

(b) Promote the integration of soil conservation measures into relevant domestic laws, taking into account, where appropriate, relevant international instruments such as the United Nations Convention to Combat Desertification in Those Countries Experiencing Serious Drought and/or Desertification, Particularly in Africa (UNCCD). It is noted that the terms of reference of this Commission on Environmental Law project on soils were drafted to be generally consistent with the Montevideo Programme III, Objective 12 "Soils".

More generally, the Programme includes not only development of international agreements, but also international guidelines, principles and standards, as well as the provision of assistance to develop capacity to formulate and implement these. In this regard, many aspects of the Programme would support a general initiative for soil legislation reform, including undertaking actions such as improving the effectiveness of environmental law on soils, improving the conservation and management of soil and forging better links between environmental law on soils and other fields of environmental law.

2.6.2 The Plan of Implementation of the World Summit on Sustainable Development 2002

The World Summit on Sustainable Development held in Johannesburg in September 2002 (WSSD) reaffirmed sustainable development as a central element of the international agenda and gave new impetus to global action to fight poverty and protect the environment.[37] Governments agreed to and reaffirmed a wide range of concrete commitments and targets for action to achieve more effective implementation of sustainable development objectives. Of particular importance to the objectives of the Guide is the recognition by the WSSD for the need to increase protection of the land as a major strategy against poverty eradication, reduce the loss of fertile soil and increase the effectiveness of use of water. The WSSD Johannesburg *Plan of Implementation* calls for the development of integrated land management plans, improving the productivity of land and adoption of policies and laws that guarantee well-defined and enforceable land and water use rights, and promote security of tenure. Framework 4, discussed in Section III of this Guide, gives an example of the type of legal and institutional system that may be considered to manage this type of integrated approach to natural resource planning.

2.6.3 A World Soils Agenda

In recognition of the need for many changes in the way society views and uses the soil, the International Union of Soil Sciences (IUSS) (through its specialist working group on "International Actions for the Sustainable Use of Soils" (IASUS)), prepared *A World Soils Agenda* which targets three major Tasks – science, policy making and implementation. It is considered imperative that the key Agenda item of each of the Task areas be considered in the review and framing of soil legislation.[38] The Guide suggests that States review the Nine Agenda items as follows, in the context of their specific legislative needs for the sustainable use of soils:

---

37 World Summit on Sustainable Development, 2002, *Plan of Implementation,* United Nations; World Summit on Sustainable Development, 2002, *A Framework for Action on Agriculture,* WEHAB (Water, Energy, Health, Agriculture and Biodiversity) Working Group; World Summit on Sustainable Development, 2002, *The Johannesburg Declaration on Sustainable Development*, United Nations.

38 Hurni and Meyer, 2002, The *World Soils Agenda* is a state of the art discussion on soils that was specially prepared for the 17th World Congress of Soil Sciences 2002.

Task 1 – Science, monitoring and evaluation

- Agenda 1 – Assessing the status and trends of soil degradation.
- Agenda 2 – Defining impact indicators and monitoring tools.
- Agenda 3 – Developing principles, technologies, approaches and enabling frameworks for sustainable land management.

Task 2 – Policy guidance

- Agenda 4 – Identifying an international, multi-disciplinary network for soil issues.
- Agenda 5 – Establishing an intergovernmental panel on soils.
- Agenda 6 – Providing guidance to develop and implement national soils policies.

Task 3 – Implementation

- Agenda 7 – Promoting initiatives for sustainable land management.
- Agenda 8 – Ensuring inclusion of soil-related issues in development programmes.
- Agenda 9 – Providing guidance for national and local action.

2.6.4 The Committee for the Review of the Implementation of the UNCCD

The Conference of the Parties of the UNCCD (COP), by its decision 1/COP.5, established the Committee for the Review of the Implementation of the Convention ("CRIC") to assist the COP in regularly reviewing the implementation of the Convention, in light of experience gained at the national, subregional, regional and international levels, and to facilitate the exchange of information on measures adopted by the Parties, pursuant to Article 26 of the Convention.[39] The objective of the CRIC is to draw conclusions and to propose to the COP concrete recommendations on further steps in the implementation of the Convention.[40] With regard to the adequacy of national legislation to manage and control desertification, the CRIC process found that national legislation was generally lacking in its ability to achieve this objective and on this basis furnished a number of important recommendations for the immediate improvement of the capability of national legislative and institutional systems. The improvements needed in the legislative systems for desertification management will also directly benefit the sustainable use of soil more generally as follows:[41]

- A compendium of laws is needed to deal with the commitments entered into by States under the extensive requirements of the Convention. The need for more coherent legislative codes, policy instruments and strategic frameworks dealing with sustainable land management emerged as one of the main challenges and opportunities for the UNCCD process, including a stocktaking exercise on compliance of national legislation with the UNCCD.

---

39 See UNCCD *Decision 1/COP.5 2002*.

40 See UNCCD Secretariat, *Report of the Committee for the Review of the Implementation of the Convention*, 2002.

41 *Supra*, Paras. 124–128.

- Incentive systems, land tenure regimes and protection codes for natural resources should be reviewed, where necessary, to integrate aspects relating to land degradation, desertification and drought, recognizing the role of the UNCCD, and to emphasise preventive measures.
- Despite the fact that progress has been made on environmental legislation, an assessment of the impact in terms of enforcement is necessary to evaluate its effectiveness. Such an assessment will clearly assist in ascertaining how legal measures have strengthened the fight against desertification.
- Law enforcement and harmonization were mentioned as a potential bottleneck due to the limited human resources available to effectively translate laws into concrete activities. Country Parties should specify their needs in terms of capacity-building and training schemes to effectively address this concern, including at the local level.

To promote sustainable livelihoods in affected areas and stimulate the involvement of the private sector in combating desertification, legislative measures should address sustainable land use rights and secure investments.

2.6.5 UNEP's Strategy on Land Use Management and Soil Conservation

This Strategy outlines the critical issues UNEP sees in environmental assessment, policy guidance and implementation to improve the integration of environmental land and soil aspects across other environmental focal areas and relevant international, regional and national development processes, in particular to meet the UN Millennium Development Goals.[42] The Millennium Goals that UNEP identifies as directly or indirectly relevant to sustainable land use management and soil conservation include the eradication of extreme poverty and hunger, promotion of gender equality and empowerment of women, ensuring environmental sustainability and developing a global partnership for development. Moreover, the UNEP Strategy promotes the "ecosystem approach" for land use management and soil conservation, and in this context it outlines:[43]

- The environmental land use and soil issues relevant to UNEP's portfolio.
- The relationship of land and soil issues to other environmental focal areas.
- A complementary UNEP Land and Water Policy.
- Land use management, biodiversity and forests issues.
- Land management and climate change issues.
- Issues associated with the impact of chemicals, industrial waste and urbanisation on land and soils.

---

42 United Nations Environment Programme, 2004, *UNEP's Strategy on Land Use Management and Soil Conservation. A Strengthened Functional Approach*, UNEP Policy Series, Nairobi; World Summit on Sustainable Development, 2002.

43 *Supra*, p. 19–34.

- Land use policy, trade and poverty reduction issues.

Obviously, more effective or improved soil legislation will play a critical role in accommodating various aspects of, or implementing this Strategy at a national level, as part of a comprehensive and integrated approach to land use management and soil conservation. This Guide recognises that various aspects of the UNEP Strategy can be effectively used to help formulate particular legal and institutional elements for national soil law, either in establishing the direction for particular elements or groups of elements, or deciding the elements themselves.[44]

2.7 Using this guide

The legal and institutional elements suggested in this Guide should be regarded as "generic". It is expected that any person who uses these generic elements would carry out adequate background research to clearly identify the principal legal, physical, cultural, institutional and socio-economic factors that need to be taken into consideration in the approach to new or reformed soil legislation. The elements, as they appear in the Guide, may need to be revised to clearly reflect the actual domestic situation, and where appropriate, new elements should be constructed to properly represent the local and national requirements, and any international requirements as they may apply to the particular State.

The following points will assist in the interpretation and application of the Guide:

1. Each element is presented with a short introductory statement to introduce its key aspects, followed by a series of statements that can be viewed as functions or activities, or in some instances may be adopted as a rule, depending in which context the user wishes to apply them.
2. Those using the legal *elements* set out in this Guide should conduct adequate background research to clearly identify the principal legal, ecological, cultural, institutional and socio-economic factors that need to be considered in the approach to new or reformed legislation for sustainable use of soil.
3. The elements as they appear here may have to be modified to clearly convey an actual domestic circumstance in a particular jurisdiction, and where appropriate, new or additional elements may have to be drafted to properly represent the circumstance encountered.
4. The Guide may be applied at different levels for the sustainable use of soil, including the national level, a biogeographical region, a river basin, an eco-region, and the local level.
5. The suggested elements are designed to help a State construct an independent piece of "sustainable soil" legislation, or alternatively, the elements could be integrated with other environmental law elements to form a broader, more encompassing piece of environmental legislation which includes provisions for the sustainable use of soil.

44 *Supra*, Section C, "Policy development and implementation", p. 41–43, paras 38–42.

2.8 Application of particular terms and phrases

Many terms and phrases in the Guide are used in a generic sense to ensure consistency in understanding and application of particular legal/soil/human interactions, in particular key legal, ecological and sociological issues.[45] Users of the Guide should consult the Glossary for an explanation of key words and phrases that appear in the Guide.[46] These key words and phrases are central to the meaning of particular elements and are fundamental to their application.

The fundamental term that underpins the structure and application of the Guide is the term, "sustainable use of soil", which means:

> "the use of soils in a manner that preserves the balance between the processes of soil formation and soil degradation, while maintaining the ecological functions and needs of soil".

In this context, "the use of soil" means "the role of soil in the conservation of biodiversity and the maintenance of human life".[47]

Other often used key terms include:

- "Ecological integrity of soil"
- "Ecological soil standard"
- "Soil ecological community"
- "Soil environment"

2.9 Specific legislative elements for disadvantaged people

It has been indicated that "some 70 percent of poor and hungry people in developing countries live in rural areas and depend directly or indirectly on agriculture for the livelihoods".[48] This situation clearly illustrates the immense challenge faced by the world to eradicate poverty and to maintain food security while ensuring the sustainable use of soil. It has been acknowledged that the sustainable use of soil is one of the key factors in the eradication of rural poverty but this situation is complicated when extreme poverty and hunger push people onto marginal lands and more fragile ecosystems characterised by drought stress and low soil fertility. The issues of poverty, food security and land degradation were thoroughly canvassed at the WSSD.[49] Many reasons have been cited for rural poverty, including: lack of access to resources and services, land tenure and distribution patterns, land degradation, social degradation, lack of education

---

45 Hannam with Boer, 2002, Section 2.

46 Hannam with Boer, 2002, Section VI.

47 Ibid.

48 World Summit on Sustainable Development, 2002, *A Framework for Action on Agriculture*, p. 7 "Agriculture: Key Issues and Challenges".

49 World Summit on Sustainable Development, 2002, *Plan of Implementation*, Section II, Poverty; World Summit on Sustainable Development, 2002, *A Framework for Action on Agriculture*; Hurni and Meyer, 2002; also Collin, R.W., 1994, Review of Legal Literature on Environmental Racism, Environmental Equity, and Environmental Justice, *Journal of Environmental Law and Litigation*, University of Oregon School of Law, 9:121.

and training and the unfair conditions of trade.[50] The WSSD acknowledges that urgent and sustainable measures are required to reduce the rate of poverty, based on effective farmers' organizations, market instruments, law reform, decentralisation of decision-making and ongoing financial assistance. Empowerment of women farmers and related gender issues, land issues, financial markets and appropriate legal systems have been highlighted as important matters for attention.[51]

In recognition of the important links between soil degradation, poverty and food security, and the steadily increasing percentage of the rural poor in many countries, a special set of legal and institutional elements form part of the Guide. They recognise some of the specific needs of "disadvantaged people" and soil.

2.10 Conclusion

It is important to emphasise that this Guide is meant to be used as a *basis* for the development and/or reform of soil legislation, policy and institutions and that the elements suggested are open to adaptation by policy makers and legislative drafters. Different geographic, demographic and land use contexts will demand different approaches. The fundamental point is that the soil environment must be considered as essential to the sustainability of all terrestrial life, and must therefore be legally protected and sustainably managed at the highest level of environmental significance.

50 See Tandon, Y., 1995, "Poverty, Processes of Impoverishment and Empowerment: A Review of Current Thinking and Action", in Titi, V., and N. Singh (Eds.), *Empowerment for Sustainable Development: Toward Operational Strategies*, Fernwood Publishing Ltd, Zed Books; and various papers in, Hussain, I., and E. Biltonen (Eds.), 2001, *Proceedings of National Workshops on Pro-poor Intervention Strategies in Irrigated Agriculture in Asia*, Colombo, International Water Management Institute; The World Bank, 2001, *China, Overcoming Rural Poverty*, A World Bank Country Study, The World Bank, Washington, D.C., USA.

51 See Collin, 1994; e.g., see *Protocol to the African Charter on Human and People's Rights on the Establishment of an African Court on Human and People's Rights*, adopted by the Assembly of Heads of States and of Governments of the organization of African Unity (OAU) on 19th Ordinary Session on 9 July 1998 in Ouagadougou, Burkina Faso; The *African Charter on Human and Peoples' Rights* reaffirms adherence to the principles of human and peoples' rights, freedoms and duties contained in the declarations, conventions and other instruments adopted by the Organization of African Unity, and other international organizations. The Charter was adopted in 1981, OAU Doc. CAB/LEG/67/3 rev. 5, 21 I.L.M. 58, and entered into force in 1986; UNEP 2004.

II. International principles for drafting national soil legislation

This section sets out the relevant international environmental principles to be used as a general foundation for the drafting of national soil legislation. They can be used in either of two ways:

1. As a basic underlying policy and ethical position to frame a particular legal and institutional element.
2. As a separate, specific State legal and institutional element, or integrated with another State-level element from Section III.

The international environmental law principles are thus presented under two categories; General Principles and Specific Principles. Each statement of principle is reasonably self-explanatory but extra comments are made in Italics where necessary. Key sources for the Principles and environmental law concepts of significance are indicated where appropriate.

1. General principles

These are universal principles that convey a basic ethical responsibility to the protection and management of soil.[52]

Principle 1

General global responsibility to soil

The world community as a whole and individual States have the responsibility to protect and conserve soil in an ecologically sustainable manner for the benefit of present and future generations.[53]

Soil is an essential component of the terrestrial ecosystems of every State and humans need to preserve and foster the basic functions of soil to ensure a healthy, stable soil ecosystem that can maintain the ever-expanding demands of food production within a healthy soil environment.[54]

---

52 In the future, it may be possible for conformity with these principles by individual States to be reported to a central body, such as the Commission on Sustainable Development; note also that *A World Soils Agenda*, p. 8, recommends establishing an Intergovernmental Panel on Soils, the objectives of which would be similar to the Intergovernmental Panel on Climate Change (IPCC).

53 See Holler, E., 1995, "Institutional Aspects of International Governance", *Indiana Journal of Global Studies,* 3, 1:121. This article discusses the issue of "leadership" and State power.

54 Hannam with Boer, 2002, p. 16–17, "Soil and the Environment" and "An Ecosystem-Based Approach".

Principle 2

Entitlement to a healthy and ecologically sustainable soil environment

Human beings are entitled to a healthy and ecologically sustainable soil environment.[55]

There is no terrestrial life without soil; it is the living central component in most ecosystems, interacting with the lithosphere, biosphere, hydrosphere and atmosphere. Soil produces biomass; it acts as a filtering, buffering and transformation medium between the atmosphere, ground water and plant cover; soils are a biological habitat and gene reserve.

Principle 3

Ecosystem approach

An ecosystem approach must be applied in all aspects of soil planning and decision-making.[56]

Soil degradation is an insidious problem, but the rate of soil degradation would be much slower if present knowledge was applied more widely and wisely. To soil scientists, the continuing depletion and removal of natural vegetation, loss of biodiversity, and the erosion, pollution and compaction of soils are clear signs that soil degradation is a threat to the quality of life on Earth. It is therefore appropriate to apply an ecosystem approach in all aspects of soil planning and decision-making.[57]

Principle 4

Sovereignty and responsibility

States have, in accordance with the Charter of the United Nations and the principles of international law, the sovereign right to use their soil resources in accordance with their own environmental and developmental policies, and the responsibility to ensure that activities within their jurisdiction or control do not cause damage to the soil environment of other States or of areas beyond the limits of national jurisdiction.[58]

---

[55] See United Nations Conference on Environment and Development, *Rio Declaration on Environment and Development* (UN Doc. A/CONF.151/5Rev. 1, 1992), Principle 1.

[56] Hannam with Boer, 2002, p. 17; *Convention on Biological Diversity* (Rio de Janeiro, 5 June 1992), Article 1, Objectives.

[57] See Taylor, P.E., 1998, "From Environmental to Ecological Human Rights: A New Dynamic in International Law", *The Georgetown International Environmental Law Review*, X: 309; Sheals, 1969.

[58] *Rio Declaration on Environment and Development 1992*, from Principle 2. Principle 2 comprises "two elements which cannot be separated without fundamentally changing their sense and effect: the sovereign right of states to exploit their own natural resources; and the responsibility, or obligation, not to cause damage to the environment of other states or of areas beyond the limits of national jurisdiction. Taken together, (state practice has since 1972 assiduously prevented their decoupling) they establish the basic obligation underlying international environmental law and the source of its further elaboration in rules of greater specificity; see, Sand, P., 2003, *Principles of International Environmental Law*, Cambridge University Press, second edition, p. 235– 246; O'Connell, M.E., 1995. "Enforcement and the Success of International Environmental Law", *Indiana Journal of Global Legal Studies*, 3,1:47, for a discussion on the international enforcement mechanisms and the use of domestic courts for international environmental law enforcement; and Berwick, 1998.

Principle 5

International cooperation

States should cooperate in a spirit of global partnership to conserve, protect and restore the health and integrity of the Earth's soils. In view of the different contributions to global soil degradation, States have common but differentiated responsibilities. The developed countries shall acknowledge the responsibility that they bear in the international pursuit of the sustainable use of soil in view of the pressures their society places on the global environment in general and on soil in particular, and of the technologies and financial resources they command.[59]

Cooperation is particularly important in the soils area, in terms of transferring knowledge and expertise between nations, in order to rehabilitate degraded soils, protect the highest quality soils for agriculture and to reduce the food deficit areas in States and regions which have caused disparities in standards of living. Adequate levels of food security need to be reached and maintained for human survival.[60]

Principle 6

Monitoring global soil health and condition

States should monitor the general condition and health of soil within their territories and inform the world community on a regular basis.[61]

---

[59] The principle of cooperation has become basic in international environmental law, e.g., see Preamble to the *Convention on Biological Diversity:* "Stressing the importance of, and the need to promote, international, regional and global cooperation among States and intergovernmental organizations and the non-governmental sector for the conservation of biological diversity and the sustainable use of its components," and also CBD Article 5, Cooperation: "Each Contracting Party shall, as far as possible and as appropriate, cooperate with other Contracting Parties, directly or, where appropriate, through competent international organizations, in respect of areas beyond national jurisdiction and on other matters of mutual interest, for the conservation and sustainable use of biological diversity." See also, Sands, P., 2003, *Principles of International Environmental Law,* Cambridge University Press, p. 285–290.

[60] See Food and Agriculture Organization of the United Nations, 2002, *Report of the World Food Summit: five years later*, Part I, Rome.

[61] Hurni and Meyer, 2002, p. 18; this obligation is similar to that found in the UNESCO Operational Guidelines for the Implementation of the *1972 Convention Concerning the Protection of the World Cultural and Natural Heritage* (World Heritage Convention) where States are obliged to produce monitoring reports of the condition of their World Heritage properties on a regular basis, Section II, "Reactive Monitoring and Periodic Reporting", cls 68–79; see http://whc.unesco.org/nwhc/pages/doc/main.htm. See also note 58.

2. Specific principles to be reflected in soil legislation

These principles cover specific environmental issues and concerns for soil.

Principle 7

The precautionary

In order to protect the soil environment, the precautionary approach should be widely applied by States according to their capabilities. Where there are threats of serious or irreversible damage to the soil environment, lack of full scientific certainty shall not be used as a reason for postponing measures to prevent soil degradation.[62]

This Principle is central to the scheme of ecosystem-based environmental management, and is particularly pertinent in the context of soil, given the risks involved in losing soil capability for many generations if inappropriate management regimes are put into place.

Principle 8

Maintenance of biodiversity

States should adopt the measures necessary to conserve biological diversity, including species diversity, genetic diversity within species, and ecosystem diversity, especially through *in situ* conservation.[63]

Given the importance of soil to the maintenance of biodiversity, a principal objective of soil legislation should be to protect and manage biodiversity in general, but soil biodiversity in particular.

Principle 9

Polluter pays principle

Anyone whose activities cause or are likely to cause a loss of the ecological integrity of soil should bear the cost of full preventive or restorative measures.[64]

---

62 As adapted from Principle 15 of the *Rio Declaration*; see Cameron, J., and J. Abouchar, 1991, "The Precautionary Principle, A Fundamental Principle of Law and Policy for the Protection of the Global Environment", in *Boston College International and Comparative Law Review*, 4:1–27, Boston College Law School, Newton Center, MA, USA; de Sadeleer, 2002, Chapter 3 "The Precautionary Principle"; note that the words "cost-effective" have been deleted here in adapting the original Rio Declaration formula, on the basis that it is unlikely that appropriately advised States and their soil conservation bodies would introduce measures that were not seen to be cost-effective.

63 See Preamble of the *1992 Convention on Biological Diversity* which recognises the conservation of biological diversity as a common concern of humankind (see Article 2 in particular); IUCN (The World Conservation Union), 2000, see discussion under Article 18, "Biological Diversity".

64 De Sadeleer, 2002; the Polluter Pays Principle occurs in a binding form in Article 10(d) of the *1985 ASEAN Agreement on the Conservation of Nature and Natural Resources*; Article 2(1) of the *1991 Convention on the Protection of the Alps* (Salzburg, 7 November 1991), not yet in force, reprinted in 31 ILM, 767; and Article 2.5(b) of the *1992 Helsinki Convention on the Protection and Use of Transboundary Watercourses and International Lakes.*

Principle 10

The principle of prevention

States shall adopt measures directed at prevention of damage to the soil environment.

Prevention forms a prudent complement to the polluter-pays principle (where the latter does not necessarily compel polluters to reduce their pollution by requiring them to internalize their costs). Preventive measures should not depend on the appearance of soil ecological problems; they anticipate damage, or where it has occurred, try to ensure it does not spread.[65]

Principle 11

Information and participation

Everyone has the right to be informed of the ecological condition and state of the soil and to participate in the procedures that assess the impact of a change in land use on the ecological integrity of the soil environment, including access to soil science information and to enforcement processes.[66]

Principle 12

Cooperation within states

Public authorities, associations and private persons shall cooperate to protect the ecological integrity of the soil environment at all levels of environmental governance.[67]

Principle 13

Globalization

States shall cooperate to promote an awareness of the need to address the problem of soil degradation in the open international economic system that is now accepted for the economic growth and sustainable development in all countries.

Soil legislation should acknowledge soil as a finite, largely non-renewable ecological element and include the procedures that enable appropriate policies to be formulated to protect the soils of the trading nations from unsustainable use. Soil environmental protection measures addressing transboundary or global environmental problems, should, as far as possible, be based on an international consensus.[68]

---

65 De Sadeleer, 2002, see Chapter 2, discussion on the Principle of Prevention; the preventive principle is implicitly or explicitly endorsed by a number of international treaties; see Article 4 of the *ASEAN Agreement on the Conservation for Nature and Natural Resources* (not yet in force) and Article 14, *1992 Convention on Biological Diversity*.

66 *Rio Declaration*, Principle 10. and Convention on Access to Information, Public Participation In Decision-Making and Access to Justice in Environmental Matters, www.unece.org/env/pp/documents/cep43e.pdf

67 *Rio Declaration*, Principles 8 and 10.

Principle 14

Transboundary issues

States shall effectively cooperate to discourage or prevent the relocation and transfer to other States of any activities and substances that cause a loss of integrity of the soil environment or, indirectly by causing a loss of integrity of the soil environment and in a manner harmful to human health.[69]

Principle 15

Obligation to notify other states

States shall immediately notify other States of any natural disasters or other emergencies that are likely to produce sudden harmful effects to the soil environment of those States.

The international community must make every effort to help States so afflicted. States should also provide prior and timely notification and relevant information to potentially affected States on activities that may have a significant adverse transboundary soil environmental effect and must consult with those States at an early stage and in good faith.[70]

Principle 16

Legal action against another state

States shall have the right to take legal action against another State for damage to its soil environment arising from the transboundary effects of unsustainable land use or soil pollution in the latter State.

---

68 See Kaul, I., I. Grunberg and M. Stern, Eds., 1999, *Global Public Goods – International Cooperation in the 21st Century*, UNDP, Oxford University Press: it is advocated that the globalizing world requires a theory of global public goods to achieve crucial goals such as financial stability, human security and the reduction of environmental pollution; see United Nations Development Programme, 1999, *Globalization with a Human Face*, Human Development Report, Background Papers Volume 1, UNDP, New York, http://hdr.undp.org/reports/global/1999/en/; Tarasofsky, R.G., 2002, *Towards a Mutually Supportive Relationship between the Convention on Biological Diversity and the World Trade Organization: An Action Guide*, IUCN, Gland, Switzerland and Cambridge, UK, www.iucn.org/themes/law/pdfdocuments/TarasofskyActionGuide.pdf; Reed, D., 2002, Poverty and the Environment: Can Sustainable Development Survive Globalisation?, Natural Resources Forum, 26:176.

69 See Okaru-Bisant, V., 1998, "Institutional and Legal Frameworks for Preventing and Resolving Disputes Concerning the Development and Management of Africa's Shared River Basins", *Colorado Journal of International Environmental Law and Policy,* 9,2:331; Chapter 8, "Land Resources", in Trolldalen, J. M., 1992, *International Environmental Conflict Resolution, the Role of the United Nations,* World Foundation for Environment and Development; Schmitt, M.N., 2000, "Humanitarian Law and the Environment", *Denver Journal of International Law and Policy*, 28:265; see also IUCN Draft Covenant on Environment and Development Article 32, on Military and Hostile Activities.

70 *Rio Declaration*, Principles 18 and 19.

Principle 17

Protection of soil in times of armed conflict

Warfare is inherently destructive of soils. States shall cooperate to develop the most effective soil protection and management techniques to successfully rehabilitate the soil environment damaged by warfare.[71]

As part of the general obligation to protect the environment in times of armed conflict, States should put measures in place for protection of the soil environment in times of armed conflict.

Principle 18

Role of women in sustainable use of soil

Women play a vital role in the management of the soil environment. Their full participation is essential to achieve the ecologically sustainable use of the world's soils.[72]

Principle 19

Role of youth in sustainable use of soil

States shall recognise the creativity, ideals and courage of the youth of the world toward the management of the environment in general and the soil environment in particular.[73]

Youth should be mobilized to forge partnerships with soil decision-making bodies in order to achieve sustainable use of soil and ensure a better and more secure future for all.

Principle 20

Role of indigenous people and local communities in sustainable use of soil

States shall recognise the vital role of indigenous people and their communities and other local communities in the management and protection of the soil environment, especially the benefits of their knowledge of traditional practices to the sustainable use of soil.[74]

---

71 *Rio Declaration* Principle 24; see Parsons, R.J., 1998, "The Fight to Save the Planet: U.S. Armed Forces, 'Greenkeeping', and Enforcement of the Law Pertaining to Environmental Protection During Armed Conflict", *The Georgetown International Environmental Law Review*, X:442; Schmitt, M.N., 2000, "Humanitarian Law and the Environment", *Denver Journal of International Law and Policy*, 28:265; United Nations Environment Programme and United Nations Centre for Human Settlements (Habitat), 1999, *The Kosovo Conflict, Consequences for the Environment and Human Settlements*, UNEP, Nairobi.

72 *Rio Declaration*, Principle 20; see Beck, T., 2000, *Using Gender Sensitive Indicators*, Commonwealth Secretariat, London; Corral, T., 2002, "Women's Sustainable Development Agenda", in *Natural Resources Forum*, 26:249.

73 See e.g., *Environment Canada*, Youth Roundtable and the Environment, www.ec.gc.ca/youth/yrte_long_e:html

74 See *The Constitution of the Republic of the Philippines 1987,* and the Philippines, *Indigenous Peoples Rights Act 1997.*

In order for this Principle to be adequately implemented, States should recognise and duly support the identity, culture and interests of indigenous people, and enable their effective participation and transfer of traditional knowledge to achieve the sustainable use of soils.[75]

Principle 21

Protecting cultural aspects of soil

States shall ensure that the cultural, spiritual and archaeological values of the soil environment are protected.[76]

Implicit in this Principle is that in many countries, soil is an inherent part of the social environment, and that the cultural, spiritual and scientific values of soil, both for its own sake as well as the life that it supports, should be recognised. Additionally, the soil is the locus of most archaeological items, and the management of human interactions with the soil environment must take this into account.[77]

---

75 *Rio Declaration*, Principle 22; see e.g., Wamalwa, B.N., 1991, "Indigenous Knowledge and Ecological Management", in Kirro, A., and C. Juma, (Eds.), *Gaining Ground, Institutional Innovations in Land-Use Management in Kenya,* Acts Press, African Centre for Technology Studies, Nairobi, Kenya; Maggio, G.F., 1998, "Recognizing the Vital Role of Local Communities in International Legal Instruments for Conserving Biodiversity", *UCLA Journal of Environmental Law and Policy*, 16:179; Nettheim, G., G.D. Meyers and D. Craig, 2002, *Indigenous Peoples and Governance Structures, A Comparative Analysis of Land and Resource Management Rights*, Aboriginal Studies Press, Australian Institute of Aboriginal and Torres Strait Islander Studies, Canberra, Australia.

76 See *Operational Guidelines for the Implementation of the Convention Concerning the Protection of the World Cultural and Natural Heritage,* Section VI, "Balance Between the Cultural and the Natural Heritage in the Implementation of the Convention"; *1982 Law of the Peoples Republic of China on the Protection of Cultural Relics.*

77 Disciplines such as environmental archaeology, geoarchaeology and archaeobotany are relevant to these aspects.

III. National legal and institutional frameworks for the sustainable use of soil

1. Background

This section sets out guidelines to identify, develop and strengthen legal and institutional systems to manage the sustainable use of soil.[78] An important aspect of the framework is the need for cooperation and coordination between various sectors to effectively address the legal issues concerning the sustainable use of soil at a national level. As an outcome of global environmental conferences and policy processes,[79] there has been considerable activity over the last decade to put into place legal frameworks to implement the objectives of various multilateral conventions.[80] As indicated in Section II, the 1992 *Rio Declaration on Environment and Development*[81] sets out a number of Principles for the future management of the environment. *Agenda 21*[82] contains comprehensive guidelines for nations to follow for the development of appropriate environmental legal and institutional systems.[83] In response, legal and institutional frameworks that have emerged in many jurisdictions demonstrate various approaches to national environmental law reform and more suitable legal and institutional frameworks.[84]

2. Research

An analysis of the recent legal and institutional frameworks for environmental management shows how technical and scientific issues can be effectively addressed by legal mechanisms, and indicates the range of basic law and policy research that needs to be done in order to develop the necessary legal and institutional frameworks in any particular jurisdiction. These include:

---

78 Boer and Hannam, 2003; Hannam 2003.

79 E.g., The United Nations Conference on Environment and Development, Rio de Janeiro, June 1992; the World Summit on Sustainable Development, Johannesburg 2002.

80 E.g., Shine, C., and C. de Klemm, 1999, *Wetlands, Water and the Law. Using law to advance wetland conservation and wise use*, IUCN, Gland, Switzerland and Cambridge, UK.

81 *Rio Declaration*, 1992.

82 *Agenda 21*, United Nations, 1992, UNEP, Nairobi.

83 IUCN, 2004, *Draft International Covenant on Environment and Development;* The covenant sets out fundamental principles for many aspects of the environment on the basis that they will be adapted by nations when developing or reforming individual laws. It specifically addresses soil: see Article 18, 'Parties shall take all appropriate measures to ensure the conservation and where necessary the regeneration of soils for all living systems by taking effective measures to prevent soil erosion, to combat desertification, to safeguard the processes of organic decomposition and to promote the continuing fertility of soils'; www.iucn.org/themes/law/pdfdocuments/EPLP31EN_rev2.pdf

84 E.g., Nowlan, 2001, *Arctic Legal Regime for Environmental Protection*. IUCN, Gland, Switzerland and Cambridge, UK and ICEL, Bonn, Germany.

- An outline of the scientific, ecological, economic, and environmental health issues of soils, and their legal context.
- An overview of the current international legal regime, with emphasis on the relationship between relevant measures in international environmental instruments, drawing together the key legal approaches, principles and tools in those instruments which could be considered in shaping a national framework for soils.
- Investigating the type of framework required for considering complex scientific and legal relationships, and setting out specific bioregional approaches.
- Discussing the role of legal principles, tools, and other elements in designing national legal measures and procedures to prevent or minimize degradation of the soil environment, including giving an indication of the elements that should be covered by the regulatory regime.
- Drawing on examples of the practice and legal frameworks of other comparable jurisdictions.
- Application of compliance mechanisms to promote accountability and responsibility to the sustainable use of soil.[85]

Research should also focus on the legislative and institutional approaches that a jurisdiction is currently taking, or could take, in order to manage soil environmental issues within the existing binding legal regime, to ensure that the specific obligations of that regime are met.[86] A framework should be developed in consultation with a variety of stakeholder groups, including indigenous and local communities where appropriate opportunities should be investigated as to how the present legal framework can promote transparent and participatory decision-making processes to determine access to and management of the soil resource.

Much can thus be gained from both field and desk-based research and the comparative analysis of the emerging legal frameworks of environmental management. This background can provide planners, legislative drafters and policy-makers with contextual information and real-world examples to draw on for a legal and institutional approach to the sustainable use of soil by a particular jurisdiction.[87]

2.1 Regulatory and non-regulatory strategies

Some States may prefer to develop sustainable soil strategies with a minimum of legal regulation, whereas others may prefer a stronger regulatory-based law.[88] In the short term a

---

85 Hannam, 2003; see e.g., Shine, C., N. Williams and L. Gündling, 2000, *A Guide to Designing Legal and Institutional Frameworks on Alien Invasive Species*, IUCN, Gland, Switzerland and Cambridge, UK, A Contribution to the Global Invasive Species Programme, Bonn, Germany.

86 Boer and Hannam, 2003, p. 161–162.

87 E.g., see The Regional Environmental Center for Central and Eastern Europe, 1999, *Seminar on Framework Environmental Law Drafting in Countries in Transition*, Jahorina, Bosnia and Herzegovina, 29–30 November 1998, Japan Special Fund, published in Szentendre, Hungary.

88 See Element "Soil Policy" in Section IV.

comprehensive soil policy may be regarded as being more beneficial or politically convenient in helping to achieve a sustainable use of soil objective than a strictly legal approach.

Regulatory-based strategy

This strategy is characterized by a predominance of elements that concentrate on:

- Development of statutory soil plans that prescribe legal limits and targets of soil and land use.
- Issue of licenses or permits to control soil use.
- Soil use agreements between the State and individuals, which set binding soil use standards.
- The use of restraining notices where sustainable soil use limits are exceeded.
- Prosecution for failure to follow prescribed standards of sustainable soil use.

Non regulatory strategy

This strategy is characterized by a predominance of elements that concentrate on:

- Education activities and awareness programs for sustainable use of soil.
- Soil ecosystem research, assessment and monitoring of soil use.
- Financial support for soil research and extension.
- Extensive use of community participatory facilities.
- Development of ecologically sustainable soil use standards and practices for self-regulation.
- Development of soil resource management, protection and incentive-based programs.

3. Short-term and long-term approaches to development of a legal and institutional framework

Following from the two strategies set out above, two types of approach can be taken to determine possible alternative legal and institutional frameworks for sustainable use of soil.

- The first approach is based on a short time-frame for implementation. It considers minimal change to an existing legislative regime, minor reforms of soil use policy, definitions and concepts, minimal changes to related laws, and minimal rearrangements of institutional and human resources. This approach will not usually provide all the legal and institutional measures needed to manage all aspects of soil.
- The second approach considers a medium to longer time-frame for implementation and involves substantial reform of existing laws, policies and institutional and sectoral changes. This approach would go a long way to providing most of the legal and institutional elements necessary to achieve the sustainable use of soil.

Following these approaches, several forms in which national legal and institutional frameworks may be developed are out below. While *based on* provisions of various pieces of current legislation, they are for the most part in the form of future scenarios for the development of sustainable soil legislation. The following four scenarios are ways in which these soil sustainability frameworks could take shape. In this context, they may also be viewed as a staged approach to the reform and development of soil law over time, depending on, for example, improvements in knowledge and awareness of the role of the law, or changing political or financial circumstances. On this basis, Framework 1 is considered as a lesser approach and each successive Framework explained in this Section involves increasingly more legal analysis and development. Also, Frameworks 1 and 2 are generally confined to working within and improving an existing law, whereas Frameworks 3 and 4 may require the reform and amendment of a number of existing laws to achieve an ecosystem-based law or to integrate a number of important soil conservation-related natural resource functions.

Framework 1 – minor amendment to existing laws

This framework involves making simple machinery amendments to an existing law to define more clearly the role and responsibilities of existing institutions to soil management. Minimal amendment can improve the accountability of the law by introducing, for example: [89]

- A set of sustainable soil objectives into the respective laws.
- Procedures that define the role and responsibilities of the administrators to protection and conservation of soil ecological processes.
- Procedures to develop a State sustainable soil management strategy with accompanying environmental protection policy.

Framework 2 – substantial amendment of an existing land management law to identify adequately the role of a state and the public in management of soil

This framework may involve the importation of key 'sustainable soil' examples into an existing law that create a responsibility to: [90]

- Evaluate and assess soil ecosystems.
- Carry out research into soil resource and ecosystems management.
- Plan and manage natural resources and land management systems.
- Develop human and ecosystem management policies.

---

[89] E.g., *1991 Soil and Water Conservation Law* of the People's Republic of China; where it has been suggested that more procedures be included in this law to implement the concept of "improvement of the ecological environment", as expressed in Article 1 of that law, as an objective of soil conservation.

[90] E.g., 1965 Soil Conservation Law *Log um landgradesla* of Iceland, to include the concept of ecosystem protection for Iceland's rangeland areas as advocated in, Hannam, I.D., 1996, *Report to the Government of Iceland on Reform of Soil Conservation Policy and Legislation for Sustainable Land Management*, Department of Land and Water Conservation, Parramatta, Australia; 1983 *Land Development Act* of Thailand, to cater for a greater range of soil and water conservation programs currently implemented by the Land Development Department but not catered for in the legislation as advocated in, Hannam, I.D., 1998, *Report to the Government of the Kingdom of Thailand on Reform of Land Development Legislation and Policy*, Department of Land and Water Conservation, Parramatta, Australia.

- Enable public participation in the development of soil policy and decision-making.
- Support and protect the rights and knowledge of people to a healthy soil ecological environment.

Framework 3 – soil management law based on the concept of ecosystem management

This approach considers soil within an ecosystem context where the terrestrial environment is the central ecological component but would link soil with water and biodiversity management responsibilities. The successful implementation of this framework would depend on the legislation being administered by an institution with skills in ecology, soil evaluation, soil classification, soil planning, soil conservation research, field education and advisory work, field soil conservation works, policy development, and community involvement. This framework moves soil management toward a holistic ecosystem function.

Framework 4 – integrated sustainable soil law[91]

The adoption and successful implementation of this framework relies on a major attitudinal shift toward management of the soil ecosystem. It would generally feature provisions to:

- Uphold the principle of the inherent value of soil.
- Comprehensively evaluate and assess soil and vegetation ecosystems.
- Develop specialist knowledge for soil ecological decision-making.
- Ensure participation of communities in land use decision-making.
- Form community soil management and advisory groups.
- Enable community based enforcement and dispute resolution.
- Enable legislative and policy review and amendment on a regular basis according to the ecological needs of soil.

This integrated framework would be very comprehensive, and would require substantial institutional re-organization to be effective. It places emphasis on elements that enable interdisciplinary cooperation, centralization of expertise for evaluation, and planning and land management. It introduces an efficient process of managing land reform and encourages more efficient relations between key environmental agencies.

---

91 E.g., *1997 Agriculture and Fisheries Modernisation Act* of the Republic of the Philippines, which is an example of a broad-based framework law to manage the complex physical, social and economic problems of the agricultural industry in the Philippines and includes, for example, a strategic approach to the identification of problems, and preparing and implementing agricultural land use management plans; see Conception, R.N., and G.P. Nilo, "Law and Policy to Manage Land Degradation in the Philippines", in Eds., E.M. Bridges *et al.*, 2002, at 404–413; see also the *1991 Resources Management Act* of New Zealand which is a good example of an integrated resource management law in which soil is a principal component; Lao PDR, *Law on Land 1997,* which includes "Agricultural Land", "Forest Land", and "Water-Area Land"; Farrier, D., 2002, "Fragmented Law in Fragmented Landscapes: the Slow Evolution of Integrated Natural Resource Management Legislation in NSW", *Environmental and Planning Law Journal*, 18:89.

Special legal provisions for disadvantaged people – small holder farm use law

A State may wish to establish legislation that provides for the specific human and land management needs of people who occupy small units of agricultural land. In particular, this form of legislation should include legal and institutional elements that clearly identify people who are socio-economically, politically or ethnically disadvantaged, and set out the obligations of government, administrators and farmer representative organizations to them. This could include creating long-term security of tenure to land, specifically stating the rights and duties of land occupiers, and adequately recognising the role of women in agricultural land use.[92]

Alternatively, the specific legal and institutional needs of disadvantaged people could be enshrined within more encompassing soil legislation or a related area such as equal opportunity, human rights or anti-discrimination legislation.

4. Methodology to develop a legal and institutional framework

The following three basic steps could be followed to develop a legal and institutional framework for the sustainable use of soil.[93]

Step 1. Preliminary

Drawing on the initial research carried out (see 2. Research, above):

- Identify the key issues of sustainable use of soil.[94]
- Identify the operational environment relevant to the sustainable use of soil.[95]
- Identify the environmental law relevant to sustainable use of soil.[96]

Step 2. Analysis

- Examine, analyse and interpret the relevant environmental law within an internationally accepted legal and institutional standard for soil. This "standard" refers to the basic legal and institutional elements considered as essential to include within the structure of an

---

92 See Republic of South Africa, *Extension of Security of Tenure Act 1997.*

93 See Hannam, 2004, p. 5–6 for application of these steps.

94 These can be compiled by firstly, defining "sustainable use of soil"; and secondly, identifying the expressed points of concern, the actions and information needs for sustainable soil. The issues are considered as "generic" to the State.

95 Hurni and Meyer; The nine Agendas in the *World Soils Agenda* can be used as a method to understand, implement and solve sustainable use of soil issues; see Table under Element, "National Soil Strategy", in Section IV.

96 The selection of a particular instrument for examination should be guided by the issues, and come from the body of natural resources law assessed as having a direct or indirect role in the sustainable use of soil in the particular State; searches can be made of various environmental law databases, e.g., World Legal Information Institute: www.worldlii.org/; ECOLEX: www.ecolex.org/ecolex/index.php; Asia-Pacific Environmental Law database: http://sunsite.nus.sg/apcel/&cls; to prepare a list of relevant legislation and instruments.

individual instrument for its effective implementation within a jurisdiction to achieve the sustainable use of soil.

- For the relevant legislation in each group: (i) "isolate" the specific articles, principles or clauses relevant to sustainable soil management; (ii) categorize the relevant articles, principles, and clauses according to which "essential element" they satisfy.
- Determine the legal and institutional profile at the national level. The profile includes the presence or absence of elements and a determination of the most represented elements and the least represented elements for each particular instrument.

Step 3. Discussion, results, outcomes

- Determine the specific characteristics of the legal and institutional profiles, summaries and patterns.
- Determine the capacity of the legal and institutional system to achieve sustainable use of soil.
- Document the principal characteristics, strengths and weaknesses of individual laws and instruments at the national level.
- Prepare recommendations for development of soil policy, and preparation of soil management guidelines.
- Identify areas for legislative and institutional improvement, and make suggestions for the legal and institutional reform to improve the sustainable use of soil.

IV. Elements for drafting national soil legislation

1. General elements

Introduction

This section sets out the various elements that can be included in soil legislation. Each element can be taken separately and used as a basis for drafting either a specific new soil conservation statute, modifying an existing soil conservation statute, or amending broader environmental legislation in order to address the needs of soil. In this section, examples of elements that can be used as a basis for legislative drafting instructions are italicised for clarity of comprehension. As legislation can be drafted either for national or sub-national jurisdictions (particularly in federally organized states), the term "jurisdiction" is used here to avoid confusion.

Purpose and intent of the soil legislation

There should be a clear statement of the principal purpose and direct intent of a legal instrument for the sustainable use of soil. It may be expressed as a single purpose or a multi-purpose statement. Such a statement can refer to the need for a competent soil organization, the use of particular strategic approaches or mechanisms, the geographic area of interest, and the setting of priorities for the protection and management of the soil environment.

Some examples of statements of intent and purpose include:

- To promote the sustainable use of soil in consideration of an ecologically stable and healthy soil environment to ensure that present and future generations will have the same or better quality of life.[97]
- To protect the ecological functions of soil for their own inherent value and for the benefit they have for terrestrial biodiversity and for people.
- The legislation will apply to all areas of soil used for agriculture, areas of soil used for non-urban or non-industrial purposes, and any area of soil that is subject to the provisions of the soil legislation under other related law.

Element

Objects of soil legislation

The objects should include a group of statements that express a policy, attitudinal or strategic position. Together, the statements should establish firm goals, targets and general standards for an administration to achieve the sustainable use of soil.

---

97 Taylor, 1998.

The objects may be expressed in a single or multi-purpose statement, but could also comprise a number of multi-purpose statements, for example:

- To ensure that soil is used in an ecologically sustainable way, utilizing appropriate ecological soil standards including values from the knowledge and traditional land use practices of indigenous people and local communities.
- To study the scientific aspects of soil and carry out ecological surveys to define existing and potentially threatening processes to the sustainable use of soil, including existing areas of soil degradation.
- To monitor land use activities to identify new forms of soil degradation in its earliest possible stages.
- To provide for the ecological management of soil by preparing a soil strategy for the jurisdiction, identifying soil ecological communities, preparing soil management plans and protecting soil biodiversity generally.
- To encourage the soil conservation through community participation.
- To promote the education of the public in the appreciation of soil ecological values and the protection and management of the soil environment in an ecologically sustainable way.
- In the attainment of these objects and the exercise and performance of its powers, authorities, duties and functions, a soil organization should take all practicable steps considered necessary or desirable to ensure the sustainable use of soil for the benefit of the community.

Element

Rights and responsibilities to ecologically sustainable soil

Every person has a right to ecologically sustainable soil. Such a right can be exercised not only in respect of the administrative acts of a public authority but also in respect of the action of any person likely to have a significant detrimental effect on the ecological integrity of soil. Key information to help decide the type and extent of rights and responsibilities can include information from the current state of knowledge of soil science, solutions that have been adopted by other countries and the provisions and principles that occur within relevant international instruments and strategies for the sustainable use of soil.[98]

Some of the major rights and responsibilities for individuals that could be incorporated in soil legislation include:[99]

---

98 Taylor, 1998; Dommen, C., 1998, "Claiming Human Rights: Some Possibilities Offered by the United Nations' Human Rights Mechanisms", *The Georgetown International Environmental Law Review*, 11:1; 1998 *Convention on Access to Information, Public Participation and Access to Justice in Environmental Matters*; Poirier, M.C., 1997, "Property, Environment, Community", *Journal of Environmental Law and Litigation*, University of Oregon School of Law, 12:43.

99 E.g., see Lao PDR *Law on Land 1997*, Part III, Rights and Obligations of the Land User, Section 1 – "Rights and Obligations of Law Concerning the Land", Article 53, "Rights of the Land User", Article 55 "Land Use Right", and Article "59 Rights of the State Organisations, Political Organisations, Socio-Economic Organisations".

- A right to a healthy soil environment.
- A duty to protect and conserve soil for the benefit of present and future generations.
- The right of access to information and knowledge concerning the use of particular soil bodies.
- A right of access to information on the ecological condition of particular soil bodies.
- The right for individuals and communities to participate in soil planning procedures, including the making of regulations for the protection of the soil environment.
- A right to participate in land use decision-making activities where a proposed change in land use is likely to have a significant effect on the ecological integrity of soil.
- Effective access to judicial and administrative proceedings including redress and remedy in exercising their rights and obligations to soil legislation.
- The right for any person or group to take legal action against another person, group, organization or government department (as appropriate) for causing or worsening soil degradation or the loss of the ecological integrity of the soil environment.

2. An organizational system to protect the soil environment

It is important that soil legislation include the terminology and functions that establish a duty of care and commitment to achieve the sustainable use of soil. This can be facilitated through well-defined responsibilities that can be spread across a number of organizations or legislative instruments. Particular "rights" and "obligations" may be established within an organizational hierarchy, and at respective levels of administration, for individuals, or for specific classes of officials.[100]

In this Guide, the term "soil authority" is used as a generic term. It can be taken to mean a single independent specialist soil organization or authority. It may also mean the "equivalent" of responsibilities and functions for the sustainable use of soil found in a single specialist organization, but administratively dispersed among a number of different government organizations (e.g., forestry, agriculture, and land administration).

[100] Hannam, 2003; see Water and Soil Conservation Law Regime of People's Republic of China which comprises the *1991 Water and Soil Conservation Law*, *1993 State Measures for the Implementation of the 1991 Water and Soil Conservation Law*, and 34 provincial Water and Soil Conservation Laws; Tran, Huong, Liu- Hsiang Chuang, and Guss, C., 1997, *Natural Resources Conservation Laws,* A Study of Seventeen States and their Selected Counties and Townships, Natural Resources Conservation Service, United States Department of Agriculture, Washington; and Krasnova, I., 2000, "Legal Protection of Soils, Russian Federation", in *Environmental Policy and Law,* 3076.

Element

A soil authority

A soil authority should preferably be an independent body with a broad range of specified functions and a dedicated budget, with the right to determine, adjudicate, control, and manage responsibilities in relation to the protection and management of the soil environment.

Element

Coordinating function

The functions under the soil legislation should be discharged in a manner having regard to the importance of the ecological protection of the soil.

- There should be an obligation on government to review the policies and activities of the Ministry responsible for soil, with a view to ensuring that they are pursued or conducted in a manner that takes fully into account their effect on the ecological integrity of soil.[101]

Element

Distribution of responsibility

The legislative and executive responsibilities to manage and protect the soil environment can be divided between different government organizations, taking into account national, sub-national or local interests.

- When different government organizations share responsibility for the management of the soil environment, there should be an appropriate mechanism to ensure the effective cooperation and coordination in the implementation of soil management responsibilities.[102]
- Where a soil authority fails to carry out the action required by law, a mechanism should be in place to either to substitute for it, or to provide for a judicial remedy.

Element

Levels of responsibility

It is appropriate that within a soil authority there is a well-developed administrative system that clearly delineates the role of the different administrative levels. This is to ensure that the responsibilities of the soil authority are judiciously distributed to enable the effective implementation of soil functions and responsibilities at the appropriate level of administration.

---

101 For example, *Protection of the Environment Administration Act 1991*, New South Wales, Australia, Section 4(c), "to require the Authority [the Environment Protection Authority] to perform particular tasks in relation to the quality of the environment, environmental audit and reports on the state of the environment", www.legislation.nsw.gov.au/fullhtml/inforce/act+60+1991+FIRST+0+N; see also Section 7(2)(b), "co-ordinating the activities of all public authorities in respect of those measures".

102 See Australia, New South Wales, *Natural Resources Commission Act 2003*, Part 3. www.legislation.nsw.gov.au/fullhtml/inforce/act+102+2003+FIRST+0+N

Example of the general functions of an environment protection authority, New South Wales, Australia, *Protection of the Environment Administration Act 1991*

The Authority has such environment protection and other functions as are conferred or imposed on it by or under the environment protection legislation or any other legislation.

(2) The Authority has general responsibility for the following:

(a) ensuring that the best practicable measures are taken for environment protection in accordance with the environment protection legislation and other legislation,

(b) co-ordinating the activities of all public authorities in respect of those measures,

(c) inquiring into and reporting on the efficacy of those measures,

(d) reviewing the regulatory framework for environment protection and advising on its rationalization and simplification,

(e) investigating and reporting on alleged non-compliance with environment protection legislation for the purposes of prosecutions or other regulatory action,

(f) establishing a database on the state of the environment,

(g) advising persons engaged in industry and commerce and other members of the community on environment protection,

(h) advising the Government on methods to ensure the integration of the Authority's pollution approvals and licensing processes with the development consent process so that the importance of environment protection is recognized.

Element

General functions of a soil authority

The general functions of a soil authority (in whatever form it may exist) could be to:

- Prepare a State soil strategy and revise it periodically.
- Ensure that all persons have equal rights of access to the soil environment.
- Periodically review the effectiveness of soil legislation to achieve the ecological protection of soil, and prepare amendments or supplementary legislation as necessary to achieve the sustainable use of soil.
- Undertake soil research and prepare information on the ecological condition of the soil environment.
- Implement a comprehensive soil education and public awareness programme.
- Involve the community in soil decision-making procedures.
- Establish scientifically sound processes to effectively monitor the ecological condition of soil.
- Undertake soil environmental impact assessments.
- Supervise arrangements for contingency planning in particular cases of soil pollution.
- Prepare and disseminate information to guide and direct public and local government authorities on the ecological protection of soil.

- Consider applications for permits and licences, and the granting, revision, modification, suspension and revocation of permits and licenses that may be required under the soil legislation.
- Prepare a compliance strategy to protect the soil environment, with emphasis on dispute resolution processes and enforcement.
- Enforce the soil legislation or any regulation made under it.
- Undertake remedial action to redress soil degradation and restore the ecological integrity of soil.
- Undertake such other functions as may be necessary to protect the soil environment and to achieve the objectives of the soil legislation.

Element

Functional divisions of a soil authority

The technical and operational activities of a soil authority would normally be distributed among a number of separate functional divisions (these are referred to as "themes or groups" in some jurisdictions). Each division would have responsibility for a number of principal programme areas. Collectively, a soil authority must have the capability to implement the objectives of the legislation. As a guide, the divisions of a soil authority may comprise a variety of functional areas, such as:[103]

- Executive administration
- General administration
- Finance
- Sustainable soil policy and strategy (national and international relations)
- Sustainable soil standards and targets
- Legal services
- Community participation
- Education and training
- Soil evaluation and assessment
- Sustainable soil planning
- Sustainable soil management and operations
- Soil information and technology

103 The areas listed are not in any order of priority or importance. In some cases it would be appropriate to add more; in others some functional areas could be amalgamated. In many countries there would also be regional administrative offices and they would be structured according to the specific type, role and functions of a soil authority; see Bridges *et al.*, 2002, Section 8, "Institutional Innovations".

- Soil research and investigation
- Sustainable soil monitoring and audit
- Soil marketing and public relations
- Enforcement and compliance (regulatory functions)
- Dispute resolution

Specific functional activities for a soil authority can include, for example:

- Soil ecosystem management activities – e.g., soil ecosystem functioning, ecosystem diversity, soil biodiversity, soil management activities, rehabilitation of soil, sustainable soil use, managing contaminated soils.
- Administrative activities – e.g., activities related to soil administration, role of soil committees, organizational responsibilities, duty of care, activities of special councils, advisory bodies, inter-governmental and intra-governmental functions.
- Technically-based activities – e.g., activities related to soil planning, defining ecological limits of use, soil zoning, establishing soil quality standards, land survey and soil classification.
- Knowledge-based activities – e.g., activities related to soil research, investigation, and community participation, education, extension activities, capacity building.
- Socially based activities – e.g., women's rights in agricultural land use, special education and assistance for disadvantaged groups, and poverty alleviation programs.
- Law-based activities – e.g., statutory rules, legal obligations (organizations, individuals, groups), regulatory responsibilities, legal standards, enforcement (monetary and non-monetary), land use rights, dispute resolution (counselling, courts, mediation, arbitration).

Element

The head of a soil authority

The head of a soil authority should have a basic responsibility and duty to ensure that key functional activities to protect the ecological integrity of the soil environment are implemented. Where the equivalent responsibilities of a soil authority are distributed between two or more organizations, a position should be established in an appropriate primary law with the power to coordinate all legislative responsibilities for the sustainable use of soil.[104]

The responsibilities and duties of a Head of a soil authority may include:[105]

---

104 In some jurisdictions, it may be appropriate to have a Co-ordinating Commission that has a responsibility across a number of internal jurisdictions (e.g., provinces), e.g., see Australia, *Murray Darling Basin Act 1993*, www.legislation.nsw.gov.au/fullhtml/inforce/act+65+1992+FIRST+0+N s12 "Powers, functions and duties of the Commission".

105 See Australia, New South Wales, *Soil Conservation Act 1938,* www.legislation.nsw.gov.au/fullhtml/inforce/act+10+1938+FIRST+0+N section 4C sets out an extensive range of powers, duties and functions of the Commissioner of Soil Conservation.

- To ensure that a comprehensive programme is developed and directed to the human issues of sustainable soil use, including poverty factors, land use rights, access to land, the role of women in rural land use, access to finance and information.
- To ensure the ongoing assessment of physical and chemical aspects of soil is maintained, including into all aspects of soil degradation.
- To ensure that programs are developed to control soil degradation.
- To ensure that the principles of sustainable use of soil are implemented through the preparation of soil management plans and cooperative agreements to rectify soil degradation.
- To ensure that a comprehensive programme of soil educational activities to protect the soil environment is maintained, and to involve the public in the review of sustainable soil strategies, soil policies, maps of soil ecological communities and soil management plans.
- To ensure that adequate research is carried out into the sustainable use of soil and results published.
- To ensure that investigation is maintained into existing and potentially threatening processes to the ecological integrity of soil and to ensure that these processes are listed by schedule under the soil legislation.
- To ensure an ongoing programme is maintained of designing and implementing practical soil conservation work programs to rehabilitate land.

Element

A soil advisory body

The term "soil advisory body" refers to a high level group of experts in soil science and related disciplines, established by legislation to advise and comment on strategic, political, administrative, organizational and financial issues associated with the sustainable use of soils.[106]

An advisory body could report to the head of the soil authority or a similar position and provide direction on such things as:[107]

- The procedure to achieve a soil environment that benefits all parts of society particularly disadvantaged rural people.
- The preparation, implementation and review of a State soil strategy.
- The preparation, implementation and regular review of policies relating to the sustainable use of soil.

---

106 See Botswana, *Agricultural Resources Conservation Act 1972*; South Australia, *Soil Conservation and Land Care Act 1989*, www.austlii.edu.au/au/legis/sa/consol_act/scalca1989281.txt s14 "Establishment of Soil Conservation Council", and s19 "Functions of the Soil Conservation Council"; Tanzania, *Nkansi District Council (Prevention of Soil Erosion and Water Conservation) By Laws 1994*.

107 South Australia *Soil Conservation and Land Care Act 1989*, www.austlii.edu.au/au/legis/sa/consol_act/scalca 1989281.txt s19

- The structure and composition of an organizational system to protect and manage the soil environment.
- The establishment and maintenance of a funding programme, including the establishment of special soil environmental funds.
- The procedure to ensure a comprehensive programme for education of the community on the sustainable use of soil.
- The procedure to ensure a comprehensive programme of research and investigation into the sustainable use of soil including measures to improve the knowledge of the soil environment.
- The periodic amendment of the soil legislation, and the preparation of special regulations, codes of practice or operational guidelines to protect the ecological integrity of soil.
- The procedure for compliance and enforcement of soil legislation and the measures to resolve disputes over the sustainable use of soils.
- The establishment of soil advisory committees to investigate and report on the implementation and management of any aspect of the soil legislation.

Element

Soil advisory committees

These are specialist committees or task forces established by the legislation to undertake detailed inquiry into specific technical, scientific, sociological and economic issues associated with the sustainable use of soils, and to recommend appropriate courses of action. Membership could be drawn from government officials and non-government experts in sustainable use of soils.[108] A soil advisory committee could report to the head of the soil authority. Details of soil advisory committees could be outlined in a schedule under the soil legislation and include the procedure for establishing committees, membership details, report preparation, duration and conditions of operation.

Specialist soil advisory committees can:

- Investigate, furnish reports, make recommendations or carry out any activity that may be required by the soil authority to protect the ecological integrity of soil.
- Make recommendations in respect of any measures to improve the ecological condition of soil, to rectify soil ecological problems, to develop and publish information on the ecological condition of the soil environment and ways to involve the public in soil decision-making processes.
- Arrange for the public to make submissions on the findings of the soil advisory committee.

[108] Tran *et al.*, 1997, Chapter 2, "State Soil and Water Conservation District Laws".

3. Management procedures for sustainable use of soil

General outline

A key characteristic of soil legislation should be a hierarchy of procedures to ensure that ecological aspects of soil are fully considered at the national, sub-national and local levels.[109]

Essential procedures should cover the preparation and implementation of:

- A national soil strategy.
- Soil policies.
- Maps of soil ecological communities.
- Soil plans of management.
- Soil conservation agreements.
- Proposals to adopt maps of soil ecological communities.
- Soil environmental impact assessments.
- Sustainable soil management works and projects.
- Soil education and training programs.
- Soil research and investigation programs.
- Community participation programs.
- Programs for monitoring the condition and status of the soil environment.

Element

National soil strategy

A national soil strategy is a means by which the objectives of the soil legislation will be achieved and outlines how the soil authority will operate as a key environmental authority. It should address the principal purpose and intent of the legislation and express a commitment and obligation to achieve the sustainable use of soil as a major national environmental goal.[110]

---

109 Examples of the types of strategic materials that can be drawn upon to help frame national soil policy materials include: CSIRO Australia, 1993, *Soils, An Outline of their Properties and Management*, CSIRO Division of Soils, Melbourne; Held *et al.*, 1998.

A state soil strategy could include:

- References to the objectives of major national and global environmental strategies, policies and treaties as appropriate, and link them to the objective of the sustainable use of soil.[111]
- A duty of care toward the maintenance and improvement of the ecological integrity of soil for the benefit of the community and particularly disadvantaged rural people.
- Commitment to the development of ecological soil standards, including the development of a procedure to monitor their implementation.
- Commitment to the development of programs to achieve ecologically sustainable soil and maintain soil biodiversity.
- An outline of the role and benefits of community education programs for soil.

---

[110] See, for example, Department of Environment, Transport and the Regions, 2001, *Draft Soil Strategy for England,* A Consultation Paper, Minister for Agriculture, Fisheries and Forestry, England, www.defra.gov.uk/environment/consult/dss/pdf/soil.pdf; Commission of the European Communities, 2002, *Towards a Thematic Strategy for Soil Protection*, Communication from the Commission to the Council, The European Parliament, The Economic and Social Committee and the Committee of the Regions, Brussels, http://europa.eu.int/eur-lex/en/com/pdf/2002/com2002_0179en01.pdf; Hurni and Meyer, 2002; Stocking, M., 2002, *Diversity: A New Strategic Direction for Soil Conservation*, Sustainable Utilisation of Global Soil and Water Resources, Volume I, "Soil and Water Conservation Regional Policies and Actions", Proceedings of 12th International Soil Conservation Organisation Conference, Beijing, China, Tsinghua University Press, Beijing; see key issues and strategies in, UNEP/GC.22/INF/25, 4 December 2002. *Land Use Management and Soil Conservation Policy of UNEP: Strengthened Functional Approach,* Governing Council of the United Nations Environment Programme.

[111] World Summit on Sustainable Development, 2002, *Plan of Implementation*; World Summit on Sustainable Development, 2002, www.johannesburgsummit.org/html/ documents/summit_docs/ plan_final1009.doc, *Johannesburg Declaration on Sustainable Development*, www.johannesburgsummit.org/html/documents/summit_docs/1009wssd pol_declaration.doc; also, United Nations, 2000, *We the Peoples*, The Role of the United Nations in the 21st Century, United Nations Department of Public Information, New York, www.un.org/millennium/sg/report/; Nkonya, E., D. Sserunkuuma, J. Pender, Eds., 2002, *Policies for Improved Land Management in Uganda: Second National Workshop*, Environment and Production Technology Division, International Food Policy Research Institute, Washington, D.C., USA; Secretariat of the United Nations Convention to Combat Desertification, 2002, *Joint Implementation of the Three Rio Conventions – Convention on Biological Diversity, United Nations Convention to Combat Desertification, United Nations Framework Convention on Climate Change.*

The nine soil agenda items[112]

Agenda tasks	The soil agenda	General issues of each agenda	General requirements of each agenda
1. Tasks for science, monitoring and evaluation	1. Assessing the status and trends of soil degradation.	• Soil degradation is widespread and severe. • Uncertainty about extent, severity, impacts. • Need data to remove assumptions about trends, thresholds. • Effects of soil degradation on agriculture, ecology, and humans. • Adequacy of methodology.	• Detailed information and knowlede of soil degradation. • Expand soil data base knowledge. • Need soil ecosystem knowledge. • Need reliable methodology.
	2. Defining impact indicators and tools for monitoring and evaluation.	• Soil degradation has multiple impacts on natural resource base, agriculture, economy, institutions and society in general. • Need to design a small number of multi-dimensional, multi-scale, multi-functional indicators to assess impacts. • Develop monitoring systems to determine level of sustainability, and monitor mitigation efforts.	• Need to develop soil indicators and soil monitoring systems. • Indicators should allow for assessment of all dimensions of soil sustainability, particularly soil ecosystem aspects. • Regular scrutiny of indicators.
	3. Developing principles, technologies, approaches and enabling frameworks for sustainable soil management.	• A lot of technological information on land use systems is not documented. • Multiple benefits not properly understood • Implementation depends on approaches chosen to make them available.	• Research, monitoring and evaluation should be directed towards developing and testing sustainable soil management technologies. • Important to look at ecological, economic, social and institutional feasibility.

112 Adapted from Hurni and Meyer, 2002.

2. Tasks for policy guidance.	4. Identifying a jurisdiction-specific multi-disciplinary network for soil issues.	• Soil issues are generally multidisciplinary in nature. • Sustainability of soils involves research issues in law, policy, social, economic, physical sciences. • Need adequate soil policies, capable of being monitored. • Soil policy should address soil degradation problems, from basic principles to multi-functional issues of soils and integration into spatial planning of agriculture, urban, biodiversity issues.	• Awareness-raising of governance systems. • Develop integrated jurisdiction-specific soil protection policy. • Institutional capability. • Compatibility of policies. • Advisory network or panel of soil experts.
	5. Establishing a jurisdiction-specific expert panel on soils.	• Soil sustainability is a central issue in land management. • Soil needs equal status with biodiversity, climate change, forests and water issues.	• Discuss key sustainable soil issues. • Synthesise soil relevant information. • Provide information on impacts of soil degradation. • Provide guidance for soil research. • Assist policymaking process to achieve sustainable soil management.
	6. Providing guidance to develop and implement jurisdiction-specific soil policies.	• Jurisdiction-specific soil policies need to be developed into more integrated instruments and applied widely. • Develop links to international policies	• Target groups for soil policy. • Develop ecological soil standards.
3. Tasks for support of implemen-tation.	7. Promoting initiatives for sustainable soil management.	• Need more comprehensive and integrated land use systems to manage soil degradation and achieve sustainable soil. • Focus on the soil ecosystem.	• Develop sustainable soil research products and initiatives. • Manage the soil ecosystem.

	8. Ensuring inclusion of soil-related issues in development programs.	• Consider the effect of development programs on sustainable soil management. • Integrated land management includes sustainable soil parameters. • Monitor and report on impact of development programs on sustainable soil.	• Evaluate the impacts of development programs on soil sustainability, e.g., effects on soil health, soil biodiversity, soil degradation processes.
	9. Providing guidance for action.	• Impact of land use activities on soil sustainability. • Soil, water and biodiversity issues not always given equal consideration in planning and decision-making.	• Availability of sustainable soil standards to provide guidance at all levels, local, region, State. • Be able to provide guidance for planning, implementation, impact assessment processes.

Element

Soil policy

Soil policy can take many forms. The procedures, functions or activities under soil legislation can produce materials that express a strategic or ethical position on some particular aspect of the sustainable use of soil. Anything that promotes a course of action to control or manage any particular aspect of the sustainable use of soil could generally be considered within the genre of "soil policy".

Soil policy can be the outcome of a formal policy-making procedure where the specific policies would include positive statements for an intended course of action, or a strategic position on the sustainable use of soil. The statements may reflect an attitude, principle or strategic objective. Soil policy should refer to the need for the review or reform of legislation, including a commitment to prepare particular types of legal instruments and the timing of such actions. Specific soil policies may be used to explain the principal strategic, administrative, technical and statutory functions of a soil authority, and how these functions will be managed.[113]

Some suggested areas for policy development include an outline of procedures for:

- Implementation of the soil legislation and how its objectives will be specifically achieved.
- Developing jurisdiction-specific ecological soil standards and how they will be implemented and monitored.

---

113 See Olembo, R.J., (Ed.), 1983, *Environmental Guidelines for the Formulation of National Soil Policies,* Nairobi, UNEP; Napier, E.L., S.M. Napier, and J. Tvrdon, (Eds.), 2000, *Soil and Water Conservation Policies and Programs: Successes and Failures,* CRC Press, Boca Raton, Florida, USA; Federal Ministy for the Environment, Nature Protection and Nuclear Safety, 2002, *German Federal Government Soil Protection Report,* Bundestags-Drucksache 14/9566; Hurni and Meyer, 2002; *UNEP/GC22/INF/25.*

- Preparing and implementing maps of soil ecological communities and how the information will be used in national planning and management of the soil environment.
- Preparing and implementing soil plans of management and how this information will be used in managing the soil environment.
- Preparing and managing soil conservation agreements made between government and land users and how this information will be used in managing the soil environment.
- Managing regulatory responsibilities, including compliance with and enforcement of the soil legislation.
- Education about the sustainable use of soil.
- Research and scientific investigations into the sustainable use of soil.
- Involving the community in the management and protection of the soil environment.

Element

Soil information and knowledge

A primary responsibility of a soil authority should be to collect, analyse and record general information on the condition and status of the soil environment. Through this process a soil authority can acquire knowledge to plan and target enforcement operations. A soil authority also has a basic responsibility to implement procedures to deter soil users from undertaking any act that may otherwise be undesirable, or possibly illegal, under the soil legislation. In this regard, soil legislation should contain:

- Procedures that enable the collection and recording of information on the condition of the soil environment, to enable efficient implementation of the soil legislation.
- Procedures that enable the community to be informed of its basic responsibilities to the soil environment.

Soil assessment and soil planning

The ecological condition of soil should be assessed at the national, sub-national and local levels. Information is needed at these levels to effectively plan the protection and management of the ecological aspects of the soil environment. Assessment is the application of scientific techniques to determine the basic ecological characteristics of the soil that could then be used in soil planning and decision-making activities at each level.[114]

---

[114] See Herweg, K., 1996, *Field Manual for Assessment of Current Erosion Damage*, Soil Conservation Research Programme, Ethiopia and Centre for Development and Environment, University of Berne, Switzerland, Land Druck AG, Liebefeld, Switzerland; Lahmar, R., M. Dosso, A. Ruellan and L. Montanarella, 2000, *Soils in Central and Eastern European Countries, in the New Independent States, in Central Asian Countries and in Mongolia, Present situation and future perspectives*, European Soil Bureau, European Commission, EUR 19723EN; Kertesz, A., 2001, "Land Degradation in Hungary", in Bridges *et al.*, 2002; Tengberg, A., and M. Stocking, 2001, "Land degradation, food security, and agro-biodiversity – examining an old problem in a new way", in Bridges *et al.*, 2002; Food and Agriculture Organization of the United Nations, 2002, *Land Degradation Assessment in Drylands – LADA Project*, FAO, Rome.

Soil legislation should include:

- The procedures that enable soil planning at each level, and the programs to implement the plans. At each level there should be a reference to the specific actions that will generate the different types of soil information, and the way that the information will be used in decision-making.

Soil assessment[115]

Procedures may include:

- Technical survey of the soil environment and soil database development.
- Evaluation of knowledge on the environmental condition of soil.
- Soil resource evaluation, soil classification, and soil environmental impact assessment.
- Preparing standards and guidelines for the use of soil.[116]

Soil planning[117]

Procedures may include:

- Soil plan development.
- Procedures for implementation of soil plans.
- Procedures to monitor soil plans.

Special principles to consider in soil assessment and soil planning

It is suggested that the following principles be included within soil legislation to ensure that the full practical, scientific and legal benefit of soil assessment and planning activities can be achieved.

- When planning or implementing any activity, which may disturb the soil environment, measures should be taken beforehand in order to avoid or reduce any risk or danger to the ecological integrity of the soil environment.
- Everyone whose activities are likely to have a significant impact on the ecological integrity of soil shall, before taking any action, take into consideration the need to properly protect the soil environment as well as the interests of (other) relevant land users.

---

115 See various approaches to soil assessment outlined in Bullock, P., R.J.A. Jones and L. Montanarella, 1999, (Eds.), *Soil Resources of Europe*, European Soil Bureau Research Report No., 618991 EN, Office for Official Publications of the European Communities, Luxembourg; Food and Agriculture Organisation of the United Nations, 2002, *Land Degradation Assessment in Drylands – LADA Project*, Meeting Report 23–25 January 2002, World Resources Reports 97.

116 See Ministry for the Environment, New Zealand, 1997, *Environmental Performance Indicators*, Proposals for air, fresh water and land; Australia, New South Wales, *Natural Resources Commission Act 2003*, s13 (a) "to recommend State-wide standards and targets for natural resource management issues". A list of natural resource management issues, at s 5, includes (d) "Soil".

117 *Supra.*

- If, in the light of experience or scientific knowledge, an action is likely to cause a risk or danger to the soil environment, it shall, in conformity with the precautionary principle, be carried out only if it will not have an adverse impact on the ecological integrity of the soil environment.

Specific provisions can be included in the soil legislation to cover:

- All actions, whether existing or proposed, to be carried out in a manner so as to avoid any adverse effects on the soil environment.
- The integration of biodiversity conservation principles into soil planning and decision-making systems at each level.
- The preparation of specific soil ecological standards to meet soil ecological objectives, and mandate their use in the assessment of the impact of proposed developments on the soil environment.
- The preparation of specific substantive standards for the sustainable use of soil.

Element

Soil ecological communities, soil plans of management and soil conservation agreements[118]

The three principal levels for sustainable soil assessment and planning are as follows:

National/sub-national

Preparing maps of soil ecological communities involves the preparation of soil environmental information on large areas of land, up to the area of the State. The objective is to prepare information at a national or sub-national scale on the patterns, distribution and condition of soil. This level of soil ecological information is relevant for broad strategic land use planning and decision-making. The depiction of different types, patterns and severity of soil degradation can be used as a basis to allocate funds to improve the soil environment.

Sub-national/local

Soil management plans could be prepared when the ecological integrity of soil is affected at a sub-national or local scale. This level of information would be used for planning specific soil management projects e.g., management of soil salinity, local watershed planning, to manage systems of land use (e.g., cultivation of a particular crop type), or to target an environmentally sensitive soil group (e.g., area of highly erodible soil).

---

118 These are generic terms that represent a particular level of soil planning, where soil information is gathered at the same scale, or a similar scale, to the scale of decision-making; see, for example, the mechanism and process outlined in Chapter 5 "Conservation of Biodiversity", Australia, *Environment Protection and Biodiversity Conservation Act 1999.*

Local/individual

Soil conservation agreements should target smaller units of land, involving perhaps one land user or a small group of land users. The requirement to develop a soil conservation agreement, for example, could be triggered through the identification of a specific soil environmental problem on a State or sub-national map of soil ecological communities, or could be a specific action set out under a soil plan of management.[119]

Element

Identifying soil ecological communities

The term "soil ecological community" is a generic term that refers to an area of land identified by mapping according to specified soil ecological criteria, and the area is an identifiable functional or spatial unit of land. It is synonymous with the term "soil landscape".[120] Other recognised forms of soil mapping that fall within the concept of a soil ecological community include the mapping of "soil quality", "soil types", "soil ecosystems", "soil taxonomic groups" and "soil resources".[121]

Points to consider include:

- An area of land can be mapped as a soil ecological community where one or more soil degradation problems occur, and where specific ecological soil standards need to be established to specify a particular standard of soil use.
- The State, any sub-national area, or part thereof, can be declared as a soil ecological community for the purposes of protecting and managing the ecological integrity of the soil environment.
- A tract of land can also be declared as a soil ecological community because of its special scientific, ecological, cultural, aesthetic, landscape, social or recreational value to the environment. Soil legislation should include procedures to identify and protect soil biodiversity values.
- Soil plans of management can be used in conjunction with a soil ecological community map to set out the proposed limits of sustainable use of soil, the measures to maintain soil biodiversity, and the steps required to rectify and control soil degradation and maintain the ecological integrity of soil.

Element

A soil plan of management

A soil plan of management can be prepared for a declared soil ecological community, or for an area of land not yet declared a soil ecological community. In these areas it would be considered

---

119 Australia, *Environment Protection and Biodiversity Conservation Act 1999*, Chapter 5.

120 See Glossary, Section VI for definition of "soil landscape".

121 See Bridges *et al.*, discussion on land resource concepts and key "soil" terminology, p. 6; Bullock, P., 1999, "Soil Resources of Europe: An Overview", in (Eds.), P. Bullock, R.J.A. Jones and L. Montanarella, *Soil Resources of Europe*, European Soil Bureau, European Community.

essential for land users to adopt a prescribed set of soil ecological standards to manage the soil environment.

A soil plan of management should:

- State the reasons for delineating the area as a soil plan of management.
- Set out the objectives of the plan and the way in which those objectives could be implemented.
- Specify the procedure for assessing the achievement of the plan's objectives.
- Set out the social and economic value of the plan.
- Specify the types of land uses that may be permitted, according to various soil ecological standards and soil biodiversity requirements.
- Specify the process for managing an existing or potentially threatening process to the soil environment.
- Show the relationship of the area of the plan to the principal catchment area or watershed.
- Set out the relationship of the plan to the jurisdiction's soil strategy and other conservation and environmental policies.
- Act as a mechanism to integrate the objectives and provisions of any existing environmental policy, or plan, into the soil management plan.
- Specify that the plan be reviewed at prescribed intervals and the procedure for monitoring its implementation.
- Specify how soil conservation schemes will be prepared for all or part of the area under the plan, including the types of works needed to rectify soil degradation and soil management problems and to achieve the sustainable use of soil.

Element

Prescribed activities

Where a soil plan of management has been declared and ecological soil standards have been prepared, a soil authority could, on the basis of an existing or potentially threatening process, determine whether there should be certain restrictions on the use of the soil.

It may be necessary for the soil authority to:

- Prohibit some types of land use activities altogether.
- Require a land user to obtain consent for specified land use activities, subject to prescribed conditions of sustainable soil use.[122]
- Specify the soil use activities for which consent is not required.

---

122 Land use conditions and guidelines would apply; see Hannam with Boer, 2002, Section IV, 2.2 "Protecting Land for Soil Conservation Purposes".

- Prescribe the specific ecological soil standards to be adopted under a soil plan of management.
- Set out the circumstances for the determination of a particular soil use activity.
- Set out the procedure to list prescribed land use activities under a schedule to the legislation.

Element

Soil conservation agreements and soil conservation areas

A soil authority could enter into a soil conservation agreement with a land user to achieve specific soil conservation objectives. The area of land considered for a soil conservation agreement could be referred to as a "soil conservation area". For each soil conservation area which is subject to the terms of a soil conservation agreement, a soil authority may arrange for soil management practices to be implemented to manage or rectify soil degradation, maintain soil biodiversity, and arrange for research or investigation into soil degradation and soil management problems.[123]

A soil conservation agreement can:

- Set out the soil conservation measures necessary to manage the ecological integrity of the soil, in consideration of the objectives of ecologically sustainable land use and the maintenance of soil biodiversity.
- Require a land user to refrain from specified soil use activities in, or adjacent to, the soil conservation area.
- Require a land user to carry out specified soil conservation activities or specified ecologically sustainable land use practices in, or adjacent to, the soil conservation area.
- Require a land user to contribute towards the cost of soil conservation works in, or adjacent to, the soil conservation area.
- Set out details of financial contributions by various stakeholders, including the State and local governments.
- Set out any other matter relating to the conservation or enhancement of the soil conservation area, including the implementation of a soil plan of management in the area.

Element

Public exhibition for the adoption of maps of soil ecological communities and soil plans of management

The maps proposing an area of land as a soil ecological community and the areas of land

---

123 Maggio, G.F., 1998, "Recognising the Vital Role of Local Communities in International Legal Instruments for Conserving Biodiversity", *UCLA Journal of Environmental Law and Policy*, 16:179; see various examples in Tran *et al.*, 1997, Chapter 2, "State Soil and Water Conservation District Laws", and Chapter 3, "Erosion and Sediment Control Laws".

proposed for declaration as a soil plan of management should be publicly exhibited and comments invited from the public. Materials in an exhibition would include maps, plans, diagrams, accompanying explanatory material and guidelines, and details of the soil ecological standards and threatening process to the ecological integrity of soil.[124]

- Plans should be publicly exhibited and all persons invited to make a submission on the draft soil ecological community proposal or the draft soil plan of management proposal.
- Upon the expiration of the period, a proposal could be referred to the soil advisory body for its consideration, advice and recommendations.
- A draft proposal may be submitted to the relevant Minister together with any comments or suggestions made by a soil advisory body, for a final decision.
- The soil legislation should enable a map of a soil ecological community or a declared soil plan of management to be amended, altered or cancelled. If the amendment or alteration substantially varies from the declared plan, the proposal could be subjected to the same public exhibition and declaration procedure as outlined for a new map or plan to seek the view of the public.

Element

Soil environmental impact assessment

A soil environmental impact assessment should be undertaken where an existing soil use activity or a proposed soil use activity is likely to significantly impact on the ecological integrity of soil. An activity of this type could be defined as "an existing or potentially threatening process to the sustainable use of soil".[125] A report could be prepared by a person (or their nominated agent on behalf of the person) who proposes to disturb the soil environment, evaluating the likely impact of the activity on the ecological integrity of the soil. The soil authority would normally summarize and evaluate the results of the soil environmental impact assessment and the final decision on the activity should take into account the outcome of the soil environmental impact assessment and any other relevant factors.[126]

124 For an example of a public exhibition procedure see, Australia, New South Wales *Native Vegetation Conservation Act 1997*, www.legislation.nsw.gov.au/fragview/inforce/act+133+1997+FIRST+0+N/, sections 24–36 (replaced by the *Native Vegetation Act 2003*, www.legislation.nsw.gov.au/fragview/inforce/act+103+2003+FIRST+0+N/ in May 2004); see IUCN-ROSA, 2000, *Environmental Advocacy in Southern Africa*, for examples of case studies on awareness raising and stakeholder support; Crow, S., 2000, "The Public Examination of Draft Regional Planning Guidance: Some Reflections on Process", *Journal of Planning and Environment Law*, 990.

125 See Regulatory Devices, in Section II of this Guide, for an explanation of "existing or potentially threatening processes" and "ecological soil standards".

126 Interorganisational Committee on Guidelines and Principles for Social Impact Assessment, 1995, *Environmental Impact Assessment Review*, 57:11; Webler, T., H. Kastenholz and O. Renn, 1995, "Public Participation in Impact Assessment: A Social Learning Perspective", *Environmental Impact Assessment Review*, 15:443.

The contents of a soil environmental impact assessment report should include:[127]

- A description of the activity (existing or proposed), and its effects on the ecological integrity of soil.
- A description of the existing or potentially threatening processes to the sustainable use of soil.
- A description of the environmental impacts that will result from the changes to the soil environment.
- A description of the soil environment likely to be significantly affected by the proposed activity, including the soil characteristics, existing soil degradation processes, and the degree and severity of the soil degradation.
- A description of the potential impact of the existing or proposed activity on the soil environment and a calculation of its ecological significance.
- A description of the mitigation measures that would need to be applied to prevent an adverse impact on the ecological integrity of the soil environment.
- A description of any predictive methods or underlying assumptions used in the assessment and the soil environmental data used in the environmental impact assessment procedure.
- An explanation of any known or identified gaps in the knowledge of the soil environment and uncertainties encountered in compiling the required information.
- An outline of the procedure to be used to monitor the activity.

Element

Soil management and soil technologies

This element covers activities of preparation and implementation of sustainable use of soil management programs. It includes specific types of technologies, design criteria, construction and implementation of soil management works and projects, and procedures to monitor their implementation.[128]

The procedures to achieve ecologically sustainable soil should be integrated into the practical soil management systems. In some circumstances it may be appropriate to adopt

---

127 See European Community, *Environmental Impact Assessment Directive 85/337*, http://europa.eu.int/comm/environment/eia/full-legal-text/85337.htm Article 4(3) which provides for certain classes of activities to be subject to an environmental impact assessment. With regard to agriculture, these classes include projects relating to rural land holdings, uncultivated land or semi-natural areas, water management, and afforestation: see *Convention on Environmental Impact Assessment in a Transboundary Context,* 1991, www.unece.org/env/eia/documents/conventiontextenglish.pdf

128 Including the development and implementation of indigenous knowledge and technologies, e.g., see Michael, Y.G., and K. Herweg, 2000, *From Indigenous Knowledge to Participatory Technology Development,* Centre for Development and Environment, University of Berne, Switzerland, Land Druck AG, Liebefeld, Switzerland; United Nations Secretariat of the Convention to Combat Desertification, 2000, *Land Degradation in Central and Eastern Europe: Proceedings of the Workshop on Land Degradation / Desertification in Central and Eastern Europe in the Context of the CCD, Bonn,* Germany www.unccd.int/regional/centraleu/meetings/regional/brussels05_2000/proceedings.pdf

an integrated resource management approach[129] which may include a range of technical and non-technical procedures for the management of soil, water and vegetation.[130]

This element also considers the development of soil scientific standards, practical limits of soil use, land management techniques to evaluate soil conservation technologies.[131]

Provision should be made in legislation for a variety of soil management functions and operations, such as:

- Organizing various types of soil conservation techniques and technologies.
- Developing soil conservation best practices.
- Designing and surveying soil conservation works and field projects.
- Conducting field days and demonstrations.
- Implementing plans for conservation, protection and utilisation of soil resources.
- Instructing and supervising land users, contractors and construction authorities in soil conservation and reclamation best practices.
- Coordinating the implementation of soil conservation and soil degradation mitigation policies and activities of government departments, statutory authorities, local authorities and other public bodies.
- Providing farm planning services.
- Providing soil-testing services.
- Providing farmer advisory services.

---

129 See Glossary, Section VI for definition of "integrated resource management".

130 E.g., see Recommendations made to the Government of New South Wales, Australia in the report – World Wildlife Fund for Nature, 2002, *Blueprint for a Living Continent, A Way Forward from the Wentworth Group of Concerned Scientists*, Australia, www.ccsa.asn.au/Blueprint_for_a_Living_Continent.pdf This report resulted in major changes in natural resources administration in New South Wales, including the introduction of the *Native Vegetation Act 2003,* www.legislation.nsw.gov.au/fragview/inforce/act+103+2003+FIRST+0+N/, *Catchment Management Authorities Act 2003,* www.legislation.nsw.gov.au/fullhtml/inforce/act+104+2003+FIRST+0+N#pt.1-sec.1 and the *Natural Resources Commission Act 2003,* www.legislation.nsw.gov.au/fullhtml/inforce/act+102+2003+FIRST+0+N, which are all linked.

131 An important source of information and analytical tools is the World Overview of Conservation Approaches and Technologies (WOCAT), a project of the World Association of Soil and Water Conservation (WASWC) in collaboration with several institutions and coordinated by the University of Berne, Switzerland. It aims to promote the integration of successful soil and water conservation approaches and techniques into land use systems worldwide. The WOCAT database contains information on soil and water conservation from various parts of the world. See www.wocat.net.

Soil conservation techniques and technologies

Soil legislation should include procedures for an agency, authority or department of government concerned with soil conservation to:[132]

- Provide a mix of technological and non-technological approaches in soil conservation e.g., socio-economic measures, and extension services, including various approaches used by indigenous people and traditional cultures.[133]
- Use statutory and elective mechanisms to implement technologies.
- Develop solutions that can be applied at the householder or community level.
- Develop a system for the appraisal of different soil conservation technologies and systems.

Element

Designing and surveying soil conservation works and field projects

Soil legislation should make provision for a soil authority to:

- Undertake field survey at various scales, from an individual holding up to the size of a small catchment or river basin.[134]
- Prepare detailed designs and plans for constructing soil conservation works.
- Prepare plans for soil rehabilitation and to improve the ecological integrity of the soil environment.
- Provide advice and assistance to users whose soil is affected or liable to be affected by soil degradation.
- Coordinate the integration of projects to conserve soil, water and vegetation.

Element

Farm planning services

Soil legislation should make provision for a soil authority to:

- Survey and evaluate individual holdings or groups of holdings to define existing areas of soil degradation, classify soil types, and determine the condition of natural drainage ways.

---

132 See Sombatpanit, S., M. Zobish, D.W. Sanders and M. Cook (Eds.), 1996, *Soil Conservation Extension, From Concepts to Adoption*, Soil and Water Conservation Society of Thailand; this book is conveniently divided into "Concepts", "Strategies", "Implementation", and "Adoption"; Lahmar *et al.*, 2000.

133 See Storey, P.J., (3 Volumes) 2002 and 2003, *Conservation and Improvement of Sloping Lands, A Manual of Soil and Water Conservation and Soil Improvement on Sloping Land*, (Volume 1, 2002, Practical Understanding; Volume 2, 2002, – Practical Application: Soil Improvement, and Volume 3, 2003, – Practical Application: Soil and Water Conservation), Science Publishers, Inc, Enfield, NH 03748, USA.

134 Bullock *et al.*, 1999.

- Classify the soil resources in terms of their potential future agricultural use capabilities.
- Decide the best long-term uses for particular areas of soil based on the best ecological soil standards available.

Element

Codes of practice for the sustainable use of soil

A code of practice can be used to achieve the sustainable use of soil. Soil legislation can set out the procedure to establish codes of practice and the special rules for particular soil use situations.[135]

A code could be used to:

- Establish specific rules and procedures for particular soil uses.
- Set out the soil ecological standards that must be applied to particular soil uses.
- Set out guidelines for assessment and authorization of particular soil uses.
- Establish the standards and measures to protect various aspects of the soil environment (e.g., cultural, historical), as well as other associated environmental values (e.g., aquatic areas, threatened species habitat, and vegetation systems).
- Set out the procedures for compliance with the code.

4. Education in the sustainable use of soil

Element

Education in sustainable use of soil

Soil legislation should set out the procedures to raise public awareness to the environmental benefits of protecting the soil environment. This can be approached through a hierarchy of education and information programs on all aspects of soil protection and soil management, including the means to facilitate and communicate this information.[136]

A soil authority should prepare and disseminate general educative materials on a range of sustainable soil issues, including:

---

135 E.g., see Australia, New South Wales, *Plantations and Reafforestation Act 1999*, Part 3, Plantations and Reafforestation Code; and Australia, New South Wales, *Plantations and Reafforestation (Code) Regulation 2001,* www.legislation.nsw.gov.au/fullhtml/inforce/subordleg+974+2001+FIRST+0+N under the *Plantations and Reafforestation Act 1999,* www.legislation.nsw.gov.au/fullhtml/inforce/act+97+1999+FIRST+0+N, Part 4 "complying development standards".

136 See GEF-UNDP Strategic Partnership, 2000, *Capacity Development Initiative, Country Capacity Development Needs and Priorities, A Synthesis*; Tilbury, D., R.B. Stevenson, J. Fien and D. Schreuder, (Eds.), 2002, *Education and Sustainability, Responding to the Global Challenge*, Commission on Education and Communication, IUCN, Gland, Switzerland and Cambridge, UK; *Supra*, Sombatpanit *et al.*, 1996, see various papers in "Implementation" section, p. 237–398.

- The basic ethical responsibilities of soil users, including the State, to the ecological integrity of soil.
- The ecological functions of soil.
- The role of soil legislation in the sustainable use of soil.
- Information on processes that threaten the ecological integrity of soil.
- The importance of improving and maintaining soil biodiversity.
- Role of a State soil strategy.
- Information on soil policies.
- Explanation of the different types of soil degradation processes.
- Information on the preparation of a soil environmental impact assessment report.
- Information on seeking expert advice on sustainable management of soil.
- Methods and techniques of soil conservation and soil management.
- Where to obtain information on soil ecological communities.
- Procedure to be followed in preparing a soil plan of management.
- Procedure to establish a cooperative soil management agreement.
- Information on access to judicial and administrative proceedings, including redress and remedies.

Element

Training in the sustainable use of soil

Soil legislation should outline the procedures for carrying out practical training and capacity building to protect the soil environment.[137]

Legislation should also stipulate the responsibilities of a soil authority to make training courses available in a variety of subject areas including:

- The role and responsibility of soil legislation and policy and related environmental legislation and policy.
- The basic functions of soil and various approaches to protect the ecological integrity of soil.
- Field methods to identify soil degradation processes.
- Understanding and interpreting maps of soil ecological communities.
- Understanding basic ecological soil standards and the ecological limits of soil use.
- Field soil conservation techniques, including the construction and maintenance of soil conservation works.

---

137 See Napier *et al.*, 2000, for many examples of capacity building and training approaches.

- Farm planning techniques.
- Understanding and interpreting the results of soil research and investigation.

5. Research into the sustainable use of soil

Element

Research into the sustainable use of soil

Legislation should establish the procedures for research into various aspects of the soil environment. The general aim is to improve the level of scientific knowledge and understanding of the soil environment to achieve sustainable use of soil.[138]

A soil research and investigation sustainable use programme could provide for:

- Development, adaptation, and dissemination of new and innovative sustainable soil technologies.
- Development of methodologies to identify soil degradation processes and to assess the ecological condition of the soil.
- Research into procedures for developing and monitoring soil policies and soil strategies.
- Research into the strategic aspects of the sustainable use of soils.[139]
- Research into the limiting factors on sustainable use of soils.[140]
- Research into effective ways of transposing the procedures in soil legislation into practical operational soil programs.
- Development of technologies for the effective interpretation of soil ecological data for land use decision-making and planning purposes.
- Development of indicators of soil ecological integrity.
- Research into indicators for the processes that threaten the ecological integrity of soil.
- Development of tools to effectively monitor and evaluate the sustainable use of soil.
- Development of methodologies to effectively evaluate sustainable use of soil research.

---

[138] Hurni and Meyer, 2002, p. 24 for direction on future research needs for sustainable use of soils; see also websites of peak international soil agencies for comprehensive information on soil research and investigation: International Soil Reference and Information Centre, www.isric.org, International Water Management Institute, www.iwmi.org

[139] Factors listed by Hurni and Meyer, 2002, include "assessment of science, economy and policy for land management; impact of participatory learning and of local knowledge; parameters and indicators for soil conservation; and adaptive capacities of farming systems and land users".

[140] Factors listed by Hurni and Meyer, 2002, include "soil degradation and food supply; climate change and soils; land use and cover change and soil degradation; soil degradation and economics; soil degradation in fragile ecosystems; soil degradation and legal / institutional settings; complementary policies for land and water uses; biodiversity and soils".

- Procedures for the exchange of soil science knowledge with other related environmental disciplines.

6. Monitoring the condition of soil

Element

Monitoring the condition of soil

States have a general obligation to monitor the condition and health of the soil environment and inform the community on a regular basis. Information should be provided to the public on a regular basis on the environmental condition of the soil.[141] The results of monitoring can be used to systematically evaluate the performance of the soil authority, which should also include an evaluation of the implementation of policies, field programs and research into the condition of soil.

A sustainable soil monitoring and audit programme could cover the following:[142]

- Establishment of suitable indicators of the ecological status of the soil environment, to be applied on a repeated basis to specified sites. Alternatively, a set of minimum common parameters could be established and applied to the repeated survey sites.
- Indicators must be sensitive enough to indicate a change within a given time frame, to assess and study on-site causes and consequences of soil degradation and identify the improvements needed for a sustainable soil environment.
- Indicators should vary according to scale (national, sub-national and local) and the type of decisions to be made from the results of monitoring.
- Monitoring and evaluating the performance of the legislative, policy, strategic, administrative, research, soil planning, soil management, community participation and enforcement responsibilities.
- Monitoring a number of important human issues, including poverty, indigenous and local community land rights, access by people to soil knowledge and technologies.
- Monitoring the rate of adoption of soil conservation technologies.
- Using monitoring programs that will generate reliable, up-to-date data on the ecological status of the soil environment that can then be used to justify improvements to the soil legislation.

---

141 See Bridges *et al.*, 2002, Section 6, "Tools for Monitoring and Assessment".

142 See Graham, O.P., 1989, *Land Degradation Survey of New South Wales 1987:1988: Methodology*, Technical Report No 7, Soil Conservation Service of New South Wales; Hurni and Meyer, 2002, "Finding Appropriate Indicators and Monitoring Systems", p. 18–21.

7. Community participation in the sustainable use of soil

Element

Community participation in the sustainable use of soil

States should facilitate and encourage the participation of the public to protect the ecological integrity of the soil environment. The State should prepare a hierarchy of community participation programs to enable any person to actively participate in the management of the soil environment, from the local level to the State level.[143]

Community participation programs and facilities should empower the community to:

- Comment on the preparation and content of a State soil strategy and all soil policies.
- Comment on any proposal to map soil ecological communities.
- Review and comment on any soil plan of management.
- Review and comment on any soil environmental assessment report.
- Establish local sustainable soil interest groups. These groups would have a specific interest role (e.g., to reduce soil salinity) or a multi-interest role (e.g., all sustainable soil issues in a particular locality).[144]

The range of potential interests and responsibilities of sustainable soil community interests groups should be prescribed in the legislation.

8. Financing the protection of the soil environment

Element

Financing the protection of the soil environment

Soil legislation should include financial measures designed to protect soil, which should be shared between the budgets of the State, regional and local authorities, as appropriate. It may also be prudent to consider payments by those who create a risk, danger or damage to the ecological integrity of soil, under the "polluter pays" principle.[145]

Financial aspects to consider in soil legislation include:

---

143 See Dugan, M., 1994, "Citizen Participation in Wetlands Planning in the Pacific Northwest", *Journal of Environmental Law and Litigation*, 9:29; Kauffman, S., 2001, "A Participatory Approach Towards Integrated Soil Management", in Bridges *et al.*, 2002; Markowitz, P., 2000, *Guide to Implementing Local Environmental Action Programs in Central and Eastern Europe*, the Regional Environmental Centre for Central and Eastern Europe, Szentendre, Hungary; Allan, C. and A. Curtis, 2003, Learning to Implement Adaptive Management, *Natural Resources Management*, 6:1, 25–29.

144 See Packer, I.D., 2002, "Application of a Land Management Model to Address Land Degradation in New South Wales, Australia", in Bridges *et al.*, 2002, *Response to Land Degradation*, Science Publishers, Inc, Enfield, (N.H), USA, p. 362.

Landcare Australia

The Australian Natural Heritage Trust was established in 1997 to help to restore and conserve Australia's environment and natural resources. Thousands of community groups have received funding for environmental and natural resource management projects. The National Landcare Program (NLP) is one of a number of programs supported at the federal level by the Natural Heritage Trust. The NLP encourages landholders to undertake land conservation works by supporting the communities to sustainably manage the environment and natural resources.

The Trust takes an integrated approach to environmental and natural resource management in Australia through its programs to improve water quality, reduce soil erosion, improve estuarine health, and improve vegetation management and soil condition. Associated benefits include skilled resource managers, communities playing a key role in their future direction, improved productivity and profitability, enhanced protection and restoration of biodiversity, and more people taking an active role in improving the management of natural resources, including those who are not directly involved in natural resource management activities.

While continuing to support existing community efforts, the Trust takes a long term, coordinated approach to tackling the major environmental challenges facing Australia. It does this by providing funding for environmental activities at a community level, a regional level, and a National/State level. At the Commonwealth level, a Ministerial Board administers the Natural Heritage Trust.

See www.affa.gov.au/content/output.cfm?ObjectID=D2C48F86-BA1A-11A1-A2200060B0A04284

- The establishment of a soil environment fund to finance public expenditures to improve the quality of the soil environment.[146]
- Key expenditure items could include the plans of soil ecological communities, preparation of soil plans of management, preparation of soil conservation agreements and the subsidization of soil conservation activities in a soil conservation area.
- Soil environmental subsidies could be provided from a special fund for soil conservation measures and projects to improve the ecological integrity of soil.
- Subsidies could be in the form of grants, loans, securities and guarantees.
- Soil environmental subsidies could be granted on application for soil conservation measures or projects.

145 See de Sadeleer, 2002; Heinze, B., G. Baurle and G. Stolpe, (Eds.), 2002, *Financial Instruments for Nature Conservation in Central and Western Europe*, Federal Agency for Nature Conservation, Germany and IUCN (The World Conservation Union); Australia, South Australia, *Soil Conservation and Land Care Act 1989*, www.austlii.edu.au/cgi-bin/download.cgi/download/au/legis/sa/consol_act/ s 9, "Soil Conservation and Land Care Fund".

146 See Guerin-McManus, M., 2002, "Conservation Trust Funds", *UCLA Journal of Environmental Law and Policy*, 20:1:1.

9. Right to information and public participation in the protection of soil

Element

Right to information

Any person should have a right of access to information held by the State on any matter related to the sustainable use of soil, but in particular on the state of the soil environment.[147]

Information on the state of the soil environment may include:

- Data in written, visual, oral, digital, or database format.
- Information on activities or measures adversely affecting, or likely to affect the condition of the soil environment.
- Information on activities or measures designed to protect the soil environment, including administrative measures, soil policies and soil management programs.
- The measures in place to monitor the condition of the soil environment.

Element

Protection of information

Soil legislation should set out the procedures and circumstances under which a soil authority should supply information on the soil environment to the public, including any existing actions or proposed actions that are likely to affect the ecological integrity of soil.

Key considerations include:

- The procedure to obtain information.
- The circumstances under which certain types of information may be protected or refused.
- Charges to be levied.
- Procedures for giving information to groups as against an individual.[148]

---

147 See Stec, S., S. Casey-Lefkowitz and J. Jendroska, 2000, *The UN/ECE Convention on Access to Information, Public Participation in Decision-Making and Access to Justice in Environmental Matters (Aarhus, Denmark 1998), An Implementation Guide*, United Nations, New York; see various State of the Environment reporting procedures – United Nations Environment Programme State of the Environment Reports, e.g., Europe, www.grida.no/soe/europe/index.htm

148 Soil legislation may also be bound by national "freedom of information"; see Environmental Law Institute, 2002, *A Citizen's Guide to Using Federal Environmental Laws to Secure Environmental Justice,* Environmental Law Research Institute Research Report, www.elistore.org/reports_detail.asp?ID=59

10. Procedures in soil environmental matters

Element

Commencement of administrative procedures

Where an existing land use activity or a proposed change in land use is likely to significantly affect the ecological integrity of the soil environment, a full environmental assessment may be warranted and the outcome made available for the community to review and comment.

Suitable procedures for soil environment impact assessment may already be provided in other State legislation and this should be investigated.[149]

The following procedures can be used as a guide:

- Soil legislation could list the processes assessed as being an existing or potential threat to the ecological integrity of soil.
- Activities that are likely to have a significant impact on the ecological integrity of soil should be subjected to a soil environmental impact assessment procedure, including provision for public comment on the outcome of the EIA.
- Where an activity proceeds that has the potential to impact on environmental integrity of the soil, this would be on the basis of a prior assessment and authorisation procedure, and subjected to prescribed land management conditions to minimise its impact.

Element

Administrative procedures

Administrative procedures should set out:

- The circumstances under which a soil authority should decide to invoke an administrative proceeding.
- The manner in which the proceedings will be conducted and the way that records are to be kept.

Element

Information for interested persons

Wherever a soil authority proposes to act under the administrative procedures, the interested persons should be informed in a manner and with facts that will enable them to judge whether their rights, freedoms and interests are affected.

---

149 E.g., State legislation for environmental impact assessment, pollution control; see European Community, *Directive 85/337/EEC, OJ 1985 L175/40: 553, 558,* which makes it obligatory to carry out an environmental assessment in the case of certain projects of public or private developers.

Procedures should be included to:

- Set out the manner in which the soil authority will inform the public.
- Set out the various categories of information persons can access.
- Outline the conditions or restrictions on the use of information.

Element

Administrative hearings

Soil legislation should set out formal administrative procedures to be followed for grievances to be heard.

Key considerations for a soil authority include:

- To give a person whose rights may be affected an opportunity to be heard.
- To give parties and participants access to information gathered. Where a uniform application, objection, comment and similar statements from a large number of persons has been made, the soil authority should request, where appropriate, these persons to nominate a common agent.
- The manner in which the facts, arguments and evidence submitted by the persons participating in the proceedings will be considered.
- How the objections, comments and the results of a hearing will be considered.
- The procedure for making a decision and conveying the reasoning of the decision.
- The procedure for making public any important and controversial issues, including a summary of the reasons and giving any objectors the opportunity to comment.
- The procedures for communicating with the applicant, objectors and any other parties.
- The procedures for judicial review.

Element

Criminal and civil enforcement proceedings

Soil legislation should outline procedures for respective parties in legal environmental proceedings.

These should cover:

- Prosecutions for breach of soil legislation.
- Access to all relevant information relating to possible breaches of legislation, through freedom of information provisions.
- Provision of broad standing (locus standi) to allow citizens and groups (in addition to government entities) to bring civil enforcement actions.
- Provision of financial assistance for individuals and groups to bring civil enforcement actions.

Element

Transboundary issues – the prevention of soil degradation in another state

As a general principle of international law a State has a responsibility to ensure that any activities within its boundaries do not affect the ecological integrity of the soil environment of another State[150] and there should be appropriate procedures in national soil legislation to implement the "common boundary" principle. Where a State shares a common boundary with another State, or States, it should:

- Cooperate to discourage or prevent the relocation and transfer to other States of any activities and substances that cause soil degradation or indirectly by causing damage to the soil environment of another State.[151]
- Ensure that any person who causes soil degradation, or does anything so as to lead to the loss of ecological integrity of soil in another State, directly or indirectly, should bear the cost of causing the soil degradation or loss of ecological integrity of the soil.
- Ensure that the interest of the public is properly observed.[152]

Element

Obligation to notify other states

A State should include procedures in soil legislation to:

- Immediately notify another State of any natural disasters or other emergencies that are likely to produce short or long term harmful effects to the soil environment of those States.[153]
- Provide prior and timely notification and relevant information to a potentially affected State on activities that may have a significant adverse transboundary effect on soil and must consult with those States at an early stage.[154]

---

150 See Rio Declaration on Environment and Development 1992, Principle 2; Trail Smelter Arbitration 1937/41; Sands, P., *Principles of International Environmental Law,* Cambridge, 2003, Ch. 18 "Liability for Environmental Damage".

151 See Okaru-Bisant, V., 1998.

152 See Chapter 8, "Land Resources", in Trolldalen, J. M., 1992, *International Environmental Conflict Resolution, the Role of the United Nations,* the World Foundation for Environment and Development; McGee, H.W., and T.W. Woolsey, 2002, "Transboundary Dispute Resolution as a Process and Access to Justice for Private Litigants: Commentaries on Cesare Romano's The Peaceful Settlement of International Disputes: A Pragmatic Approach (2000)", *UCLA Journal of Environmental Law and Policy*, 20:109.

153 See Rio Declaration Principle 18.

154 See Rio Declaration Principle 19.

Element

Resolution of transboundary soil degradation disputes

Where applicable, a State should include procedures in soil legislation to:

- Resolve a dispute through a formal dispute resolution process.
- Take legal action against another State for damage to its soil environment arising from the transboundary effects of soil use in the latter State.[155]

11. Regulatory devices

Element

Existing or potentially threatening processes to the sustainable use of soil

In this Guide a reference to an "existing or potentially threatening process" – means "a process that is applied to the soil or any other part of the ecosystem, which is or has the capability to threaten the ecological integrity of the soil". The "ecological integrity of soil" is further defined as "preserving the wholeness of ecosystems, including the prevention of loss of wholeness, so as to stop the commencement of soil degradation, and to control existing soil degradation, and to protect and manage soil for its sustainable use". It is suggested that these concepts, or similar concepts, be incorporated within soil legislation to draw attention to the fact that individual actions, or a series of independent actions, or a number of actions conjointly, may cause or exacerbate soil degradation and therefore lead to a loss of the ecological integrity of soil.[156]

Soil legislation should contain procedures:

- To identify existing or potentially threatening processes to the ecological integrity of soil.
- To inform the public about existing or potentially threatening processes to the ecological integrity of soil.
- To control an existing soil use situation or proposed change to an existing soil use situation where there is an existing or potentially threatening process. This may include provision for applications to be submitted to a soil authority for approval to undertake particular activities that may involve existing or potentially threatening processes.

---

155 See O'Connell, M.E., 1995, "Enforcement and the Success of International Environmental Law", *Indiana Journal of Global Legal Studies*, 3, 1:47, for a discussion on the international enforcement mechanisms and the use of domestic courts for international environmental law enforcement; McGee and Woolsey, 2002.

156 See discussion on "Keeping Agricultural Land Rural", p. 175–180, and "Protecting the Quality of Agricultural Land", p. 180–185, in Grossman, M.R., "Agricultural Land-use Law in the United States", in *Agrarian Law in the Western World*, Grossman, M.R., and W. Brussaard, 1992, Eds., C.A.B. International, Wallingford, UK, p. 171–195.

- To publicly advertise particular soil use proposals where authorization is required to undertake an activity listed as an existing or a potentially threatening process to the soil environment.
- To hold a public hearing if the comments and objections on the application raise important and controversial issues on the sustainable use of soil.
- For ecological soil standards to be applied where appropriate.

Matters to consider in the declaration of an existing or potentially threatening process

The procedure for declaring an existing or potentially threatening process should:

- Adequately define the concept of an existing or potentially threatening process.
- Establish the criteria and characteristics of an existing or potentially threatening process. These may include, for example:
  - Any method or technique of soil use (e.g., a method or technique of cultivation, grazing animal or machinery or chemical additive to the soil or to vegetation).
  - A type of soil planning technique or specific form of soil use activity.[157]
  - Any mechanical process, chemical process or firing or burning of vegetation that may significantly affect the ecological integrity of soil.
  - Known activities of soil pollution or contamination.

Any other process declared under soil legislation as existing or potentially threatening to the ecological integrity of soil.

- Processes that are declared as existing or potentially threatening to the ecological integrity of soil should be notified under soil legislation through a formal listing procedure schedule or by making a regulation.

Element

Ecological soil standards

The Glossary in Section VI defines an "ecological soil standard" as a process for maintaining or improving the ecological integrity of soil. This is a generic concept that paves the way for any positive form of action or activity to be taken that will lead to the sustainable use of soil.

Soil legislation could provide for ecological soil standards in a number of ways:[158]

- To establish ecological soil standards to protect soil against degradation, the loss of its principal functions and the loss of ecological integrity of soil.
- To establish ecological soil standards for the State as a whole.

---

157 See Element, "Soil Conservation Techniques and Technologies" above.

158 E.g., see Australia, New South Wales *Natural Resources Commission Act 2003*, s 13(a) in relation to preparing State soil standards.

- To enshrine ecological soil standards in regulations.
- To ensure that ecological soil standards are considered in decision-making procedures that affect the soil environment.
- To specify the type and degree of soil use over a specified period of time.
- To ensure ecological soil standards take into account the extent, degree and severity of soil degradation.
- To ensure that ecological soil standards consider the state of soil scientific knowledge.
- To ensure that ecological soil standards have the capability to protect the ecological aspects of soil (taking into account the sensitivity of the local soil environment and the existing or intended land use).

Element

Substantive ethical principles for the sustainable use of soil

To assist a soil authority make fair and just decisions as to what may or may not constitute an acceptable use of soil, the soil legislation should include a list of statements of principle in regard to the nature of soil use.

The following principles could be listed in the soil legislation:

- Soil use activities should be carried out according to the principle of "sustainable use of soil".[159]
- Existing activities should not be expanded or otherwise modified if they do not meet prescribed ecological soil standards or if the modification is likely to cause a significant effect on the soil environment.
- Any activity that will disturb the soil environment should not be undertaken unless all reasonable protective measures are undertaken.
- Protective measures should be based on the best available soil conservation technologies.
- Soil protection measures that are compatible with ecological soil standards are presumed to be reasonable. This presumption can be overturned if it is demonstrated in a specific case that additional protective measures can be taken within the above framework.

Element

Procedure for notification of an existing or potentially threatening process

The following procedure can be adopted as a guide:

- A soil authority has the responsibility for preparing and maintaining a set of criteria by which the eligibility of an existing or potentially threatening process can be determined for listing.

159 Hannam with Boer, 2002, Section II.

- An order could be made under soil legislation to list an existing or potentially threatening process.
- The list could be extended, amended or repealed, as appropriate.
- An existing or potentially threatening process would be eligible for listing if it meets the criteria specified in the legislation.
- Any person, the soil advisory committee, or a soil advisory body could nominate an existing or potentially threatening process and a soil authority should consider it under the specified criteria.

Element

Flexibility

On the understanding that soil conservation technologies are constantly evolving and improving it is appropriate that soil legislation include a provision that recognises the dynamics of technology:

- In areas where the ecological soil standards have been improved over time, an alternative soil use could be authorized if it does not cause loss of ecological integrity of the soil.
- Steps should be taken to progressively reduce the type and extent of soil degradation and improve the condition of the soil environment.

Element

Soil pollution

With the increasing risk of soil degradation from soil pollution, including contamination, the sealing of soil from the lateral flow of a spilled substance (e.g. oil), it is appropriate that soil legislation contain provisions to control this form of soil degradation.[160]

Specific provisions should be included in soil legislation to:

- Protect the ecological integrity of soil against dangers from the production, storage, use, spillage and disposal of particular hazardous substances, hazardous preparations or products that contain or may release a hazardous substance, including animal wastes.
- Hazardous substances and products that contain or may release a hazardous substance to the soil environment could be classified by regulations into appropriate risk categories.

---

160 See, Turner, J.H., 1999, "Model State Regulations Governing the Land Application of Petroleum-Contaminated Soils", *South Carolina Environmental Law Journal,* 8,1:1; Siegel, J.V., 2002, "Negotiating for Environmental Justice: Turning Polluters into 'Good Neighbors' through Collaborative Bargaining", *New York Environmental Law Journal*, 10:147.

Element

Control of an activity that is potentially threatening to the soil environment

The procedures to control an activity that is potentially threatening to the soil environment could be based on the following principles:

- A person who intends to commence an activity that is potentially threatening to the ecological integrity of the soil environment should be subject to controls by a soil authority. A control can be in the form of an authorization, notification or power to prohibit or limit the relevant activity.
- If a soil authority considers that an activity may cause a threat to the ecological integrity of the.g.e soil environment, a soil authority should not authorize the activity.
- The conditions under which an activity is, or is potentially, threatening to the ecological integrity of soil is subject to control by a soil authority should be detailed in the legislation.

Element

Authorization of activities which are a threat to the ecological integrity of soil

Activities that are threatening to the ecological integrity of the soil environment, especially those activities that require a soil environmental impact assessment, should be subject to an authorization.

The following procedure is a guide:

- The authorization of a new activity or the significant modification of an existing activity should only be granted if:
  - The activity will not cause or exacerbate soil degradation or loss of integrity of the soil environment.
  - The soil user has taken all reasonable measures to protect the ecological integrity of soil, including the application of best available soil conservation technology.
  - Ecological soil standards have been considered and applicable standards and technical requirements have been complied with.
  - Where a proposed soil use activity is subject to a soil environmental impact assessment, the authorization should not be granted if the site or the soil use activity, considering the results of the soil environmental impact assessment, is contrary to the public interest.

Element

Authorization of soil pollution activities

Activities that are liable to cause soil pollution should be subject to an authorization.

- An authorization to conduct an activity on the soil environment which is regarded as a potential soil pollution activity, should only be granted if:
  - The activity will not affect the ecological integrity of the soil environment.
  - The activity does not cause risks to groundwater quality or unreasonable risks to the ecological integrity of the soil environment.

Element

Notification

An existing or potentially threatening activity to the soil environment, including a soil pollution activity that is potentially harmful to the ecological integrity of the soil, should be notified to the soil authority which should be empowered to prohibit or restrict the relevant activity.

Soil legislation should outline:

- The procedure for notification.
- The type or class of person with an obligation to notify.
- The general obligations on soil users for notifying a soil authority.
- The manner in which notification will take place.

Element

Activities exempt from authorization or notification

Procedures should be set out in soil legislation to cover the following circumstances:

- An activity carried out on the soil environment that is not subject to an authorization or notification should nevertheless be conducted in a manner with the objectives of the sustainable use of soil.
- Residual substances in the soil environment from a polluting activity should be properly disposed of, and relevant requirements under pollution control legislation should be complied with.

Element

Modification, suspension or revocation of authorization

The requirements for authorized activities should be made more stringent if it appears that the relevant activity will be a danger to the ecological integrity and sustainable use of soil.

12. Enforcement

Enforcement can take a variety of approaches to ensure that the legislation is complied with at a desired level or standard. Compliance may be in the form of a direct obligation or a prescribed standard of behaviour or through a legal notice or order. Legislation should set out the procedures for enforcement, and regulate certain activities that are not beneficial to the sustainable use of soil. Enforcement functions may include responsibilities to identify particular types of offences, investigate certain matters, gather evidence, take direct remedial action, confiscate certain items and initiate prosecution proceedings. Legislation normally sets out the range and limits of monetary penalty for specified offences, as well as appeal provisions.[161]

Element

Surveillance responsibilities

Early detection of unacceptable forms of behaviour can either prevent or minimize damage to the soil environment. It may also assist a soil authority with enforcement actions at a later stage.

Procedures should be available to:

- Give government officials the responsibility to monitor the provisions of the soil legislation.
- Appoint government officials to carry out surveillance and monitoring activities.
- Ensure that government officials have appropriate powers to enter land, investigate, sample, measure, photograph, or demand to inspect items necessary for compliance with soil legislation.

13. Sanctions and enforcement measures

Element

Compliance

Soil legislation should contain powers that enable a soil authority to take action against a person or a corporation for non-compliance with the provisions of the legislation.

Appropriate powers may include:[162]

- To modify or revoke an authorization.
- To determine the legal obligations by administrative decision.
- To prohibit or limit an existing or potentially threatening process to the ecological integrity of the soil environment.

---

161 See Keohane, N.O., R.L. Revesz and R.N. Stavins, 1998, "The Choice of Regulatory Instruments in Environmental Policy", *The Harvard Environmental Law Review*, 22:313; Fiorino, D.J., 1999, "Rethinking Environmental Regulation: Perspectives on Law and Governance", *The Harvard Environmental Law Review*, 23:441.

162 This power should also extend over a corporation and the directors.

- To require remedial action to restore the soil environment.
- To stop a particular activity and require compliance with specified conditions or standards.
- In deciding on compliance measures, a soil authority should consider the interests of the affected person but also the protection of the soil environment in relation to the local area and to the State.
- A soil authority should not withdraw a permit or exemption without giving the person concerned the opportunity to comply with the terms of the permit or exGemption.

Element

Interim measures to protect the soil environment

A soil authority should have the power to implement soil conservation measures or works to prevent or limit further adverse effects on the ecological integrity of soil, including a power to stop an activity.

The procedures should:

- Enable a soil authority to enter land and undertake soil conservation remedial measures and works to restore the ecological integrity of soil and prevent damage to the soil environment.
- Specify that this power can be used only after the person or persons concerned have been warned in writing and are given the opportunity to fulfil their obligations within a specified period.
- Allow the affected person or persons to lodge an appeal to a court or other appropriate tribunal within a specified time.

Element

Administrative sanctions

Soil legislation should include procedures that empower a soil authority to apply a sanction, in the form of a warning letter, an administrative fine, an order for remediation of land or loss of a licence or permit for an activity in relation to soil.

- Where an administrative fine is imposed, there should be procedures to determine an appropriate level of penalty and to justify its imposition. The amount imposed should be in reasonable proportion to the extent of the damage done as well as the intended impact of the imposition of a penalty.

Element

Criminal and civil proceedings

Soil legislation should enable a soil authority to initiate criminal and civil proceedings.[163]

- A fine or a gaol term, or both, should be made available to punish any person who intentionally or negligently violates soil legislation, particularly where a violation significantly affects the ecological integrity of soil, or causes serious damage to human health, property and natural heritage. Alternatively a community service order could be imposed.[164]

Element

Applications for administrative and criminal proceedings

- Any person should be able to request a soil authority to commence action for administrative or criminal proceedings.

Element

Civil liability

Soil legislation should include procedures for civil liability:

- Rules should drafted on civil liability and compensation for damage to the soil environment.
- The legislation should provide for any person on their own behalf or on behalf of a group to be able to bring an action to remedy or restrain a breach of the soil legislation.
- The availability of legal aid to enable individuals and groups to bring proceedings.

14. Dispute resolution

Element

Dispute resolution and courts

In addition to administrative, civil and criminal proceedings, there should be formal procedures in soil legislation to resolve disputes over access to soil and the circumstances of soil use.[165]

163 *Protocol to the African Charter on Human and People's Rights on the Establishment of an African Court on Human and People's Rights*, December 2003. The *African Charter on Human and Peoples' Rights* reaffirms adherence to the principles of human and peoples' rights, freedoms and duties contained in the declarations, conventions and other instruments adopted by the Organization of African Unity, and other international organizations. Under Article 3(1) of the Protocol, the jurisdiction of the Court shall extend to all cases and disputes submitted to it concerning the interpretation and application of the Charter, this Protocol and any other relevant Human Rights instrument ratified by the States concerned. Further, in the event of a dispute (Article 3(2)), the Court shall decide as to whether the Court has jurisdiction.

164 Such orders are sometimes used as an alternative to a fine in a variety of jurisdictions; they involve tasks carried out on a periodic basis as a contribution to a community, and are often related to the nature of the offence.

165 Poirier, 1997; Markell, D.L., 2000, "The Role of Deterrence-Based Enforcement in a 'Reinvented' State/Federal Relationship: The Divide Between Theory and Reality", *The Harvard Environmental Law Review*, 24:1.

Mediation facilities should be available as an alternative to court action to resolve disputes.[166]

Procedures can outline:

- The role and responsibility of a court in relation to the hearing and settlement of disputes over access to and use of soil.
- How individuals may obtain access to the court.
- The rules for a court to follow in adjudication of soil disputes.
- Fair and equitable discussions, disclosures and submissions in relation to any dispute over the sustainable use of soil.
- The appointment of a mediator conversant with special needs of the soil environment.

15. Making regulations for the sustainable use of soil

Element

Soil legislation should include provisions that:

- Enable a soil authority to make regulations to manage soil on a sustainable basis.
- Enable a code of practice to be drafted that sets out the criteria for specifying ecological soil standards, including criteria for listing existing and potentially threatening processes to the ecological integrity of soil.
- Enable the preparation of special guidelines in relation to any matter pertaining to the sustainable use of soil and the role, responsibilities, rights and needs of people.

---

166 See Harashina, S., 1995, "Environmental Dispute Resolution Process and Information Exchange", *Environmental Impact Assessment Review*, 15:69; Rive, V., 1997, "Resolving Conflict by Consensus: Environmental Mediation under the Resource Management Act 1991", *New Zealand Journal of Environmental Law*, 1:201.

V. Selected legal and institutional elements for disadvantaged people

In many regions of the world, a significant number of farmers occupy small plots of land, often with minimal user rights.[167] It is appropriate in these regions that soil legislation include legal and institutional elements that focus on human rights, resource rights, security of land tenure, and flexibility in small holder land use.[168] The legal and institutional elements should focus on providing long-term security of tenure for occupiers of land, and where possible through the joint efforts of occupiers, land owners and government bodies.[169] The law should also extend the rights of occupiers while giving due recognition to the rights, duties and legitimate interests of owners. It should also make special provision to protect small holder land users from eviction, as vulnerable occupiers, and ensure that they are not discriminated against.

For the purposes of this Guide, people who need the benefit of these forms of legal protection are referred to as "disadvantaged" people.[170] They are typically people who are engaged in, or who directly use the soil for agriculture, and who for various reasons may be deprived of a reasonable standard of living, access to information, knowledge, health, education, opportunities, access to markets, and other services and benefits, by virtue of their socio-economic, cultural, ethnic or locational circumstances. Often, disadvantaged people can be a distinct community of people in a particular geographic location. They can include:

- People who live and farm in a traditional manner.
- Indigenous people who live close to the land.[171]

---

167 See World Bank Country Study, China, 2001; Hannam 2003.

168 See definition in Section I.

169 See e.g., Republic of South Africa, *Extension of Security of Tenure Act 1997*; Posey, D.A., 1996, *Traditional Resource Rights, International Instruments for Protection and Compensation for Indigenous Peoples and Local Communities*, IUCN, Gland, Switzerland, and Cambridge, UK: Nettheim *et al.*, 2002; see also Slatter, M., and D. Round, "The Agrarian Land Law of New Zealand" in Grossman, M.R., and W. Brussaard, 1992, Eds., *Agrarian Law in the Western World*, C.A.B. International, Wallingford, UK., p. 234–53, for a discussion on the role of the Treaty of Waitangi and rights of the Maori people in agricultural land use and management in New Zealand. See in particular, the role of the Waitangi Tribunal (established under the *Treaty of Waitangi Act 1975*) to investigate Maori grievances.

170 "Disadvantaged people" would normally constitute a group of people. They may be a particular societal class, refugees, ethnicity, or their disadvantaged situation may be a function of geographic locality where the poor physical capability of the land leads to a lower socio-economic capability, e.g., a remote mountain environment; see Cohan, J.A., 2002, "Environmental Rights of Indigenous Peoples under the Alien Tort Claims Act, the Public Trust Doctrine and Corporate Ethics, and Environmental Dispute Resolution", *UCLA Journal of Environmental Law and Policy*, 20:133.

171 See Cohan, J.A., 2002, "Environmental Rights of Indigenous Peoples under the Alien Tort Claims Act, the Public Trust Doctrine and Corporate Ethics, and Environmental Dispute Resolution", *UCLA Journal of Environmental Law and Policy*, 20:133; Waters, L., 2002, "Indigenous Peoples and the Environment: Convergence from a Nordic Perspective", *UCLA Journal of Environmental Law*, 20:237.

- Socio-economically disadvantaged people, especially poverty stricken people.
- People disadvantaged through a lack of access to information, education and training.
- People of refugee status.
- Women.

Such groups will often require special attention and action by governments to ensure that they have a fair and equitable right to basic human necessities and needs including:

- Access to soil of a quality suitable for farming.
- Access to water of a quality suitable for domestic and agricultural purposes.
- Security of land tenure, to engage in agriculture in the capacity of legal owners or as legal occupiers of land.[172]

The following elements may be used as a guide for inclusion in the soil legislation to address the needs of disadvantaged people, in conjunction with the main set of elements set out in Section IV, above.

1. General elements

Element

Objectives and Intent

The legislation should contain a sufficiently broad range of objectives to address the widely varying circumstances of disadvantaged people, including:

- To ensure that "disadvantaged people" are adequately recognized by the law.
- To ensure that legislation provides equality for all types and classes of people.
- To ensure that the legal framework has the capacity to support traditional and indigenous institutions and mechanisms and enable specialized knowledge to be generated for the sustainable use of soil.
- To recognise traditional and indigenous community-based property rights.
- To recognise the basic right of disadvantaged people to a healthy and sustainable soil environment, including:
  - The use of special approaches to secure access to soil resources, while protecting the ecological integrity of the soil.
  - The identification, evaluation and integration of innovative technologies and land use systems for disadvantaged people in national land use systems.

---

[172] See Tobin, B., and K. Swiderska, 2001, *Speaking in Tongues: Indigenous Participation in the Development of a sui generis regime to Protect Traditional Knowledge in Peru*, International Institute for Environment and Development, London, UK.

- The adaptability and transferability of practices to assist the poorest people.
- To enable the development of tools, concepts and technologies to ensure that disadvantaged people can farm smallholdings profitably and in a sustainable manner.
- The provision for a multidisciplinary approach to identify and evaluate low-cost technologies and devices for the sustainable use of soil.
- The institutional capacity to deal with the soil management issues of disadvantaged people and with the ability to adopt low-cost innovative systems.

The Philippines, Republic Act No 8371

The *Indigenous Peoples Rights Act 1997*, No 8371 The Philippines Section 3h), defines "Indigenous Cultural Communities/Indigenous Peoples" as:

"A group of people or homogenous societies identified by self-ascription and ascription by other[s], who have continuously lived as an organized community on communally bounded and defined territory, and who have, under claims of ownership since time immemorial, occupied, possessed customs, tradition and other distinctive cultural traits, or who have, through resistance to political, social and cultural inroads of colonization, non-indigenous religions and culture, become historically differentiated from the majority of Filipinos. ICCs/IPs shall likewise include peoples who are regarded as indigenous on account of their descent from the populations which inhabited the country, at the time of conquest or colonization, or at the time of inroads of non-indigenous religions and cultures, or the establishment of present state boundaries, who retain some or all of their own social, economic, cultural and political institutions, but who may have been displaced from their traditional domains or who may have resettled outside their ancestral domains".

Element

Obligation to recognise disadvantaged people

States have a basic obligation to give proper recognition to disadvantaged persons or a group of disadvantaged people who are engaged in use of the soil or who wish to engage in the use of soil for their sustained and related livelihood. Provision should be made for the rights of disadvantaged people:

- Within the national Constitution or within another related human rights legal instrument or law.
- By inserting appropriate provisions in any other law related to the use of soil, that will assist the objective of providing adequate rights for disadvantaged people, e.g., law relating to land administration, land tenure, water, forests, environmental planning.

Responsibilities of administrators

Obligations to the special needs and basic rights of disadvantaged people to the sustainable use of soil should be clearly stated within the respective administrative levels in soil legislation, including:

- Under the general responsibilities of a soil authority.
- For the head of a soil authority.
- For a soil advisory body.
- For a soil advisory committee.

Element

Women's rights

States should ensure that the particular role of women in the sustainable use of soil receives adequate legal recognition and protection, with appropriate support facilities, including:[173]

- Recognizing the comprehensive range of duties and responsibilities women perform under traditional and customary law.
- The need for special assistance programs for receiving information, education, and technical support for managing the soil environment.
- The right to own land, or to legal occupancy.
- The right to enter into legal agreements on the use of soil.
- The procedure for participating in soil planning and decision-making processes.
- Rights to obtain finance and secure loans.

2. Protection and security for occupiers and owners

Element

Measures to facilitate long-term security of tenure for occupiers

A variety of provisions would be needed in legislation to ensure that disadvantaged people are assured long-term security of tenure to land and legal access to the soil. Special measures in the soil legislation can include:[174]

- A facility for government to make grants to improve the livelihood of disadvantaged people.
- Procedures to develop special land use planning and management technologies for disadvantaged people.
- Use of land zoning techniques that give proper legal recognition and protection to small

[173] See Beck, T., 2000, *Using Gender Sensitive Indicators*, Commonwealth Secretariat, London; Corral, T., 2002, "Women's Sustainable Development Agenda", in *Natural Resources Forum*, 26:249.

[174] See World Bank Country Study, China, 2001, Chapter 3 "Poverty Reductions Programs in China", and Annex 5 "Policies for Poverty Reduction in China".

area land use systems.[175]

- Procedures for special research needs and methods of generating and imparting sustainable soil knowledge to disadvantaged people for the long-term use of the soil environment.

Element

Availability of financial assistance and subsidies for small holder land development

Special financial provisions to assist disadvantaged people include:

- Access to financial subsidies, grants, and low interest loans.
- Access to financial assistance for water development purposes.
- Access to financial assistance for soil and land development purposes.

Element

Rights and duties of occupiers

The right and duties of the occupiers need to be clearly set out, and in relation to:

- The different classes and types of people and categories of occupiers.
- Achieving security of tenure.
- The period of tenancy (short term, long term).
- The liability of occupiers.
- The right of access to soil.
- The right of access to water.
- The right of access to health and education facilities.
- A duty to use soil in a sustainable manner.
- A duty to implement particular measures and technologies to protect the soil environment.
- Special cultural considerations and legal protection for traditional ways.[176]

---

175 Various options may include: designating specific areas for the purposes of special types of "organic farming systems"; designating areas for the purposes of raising particular types of crops; designating areas for particular types of small area land husbandry.

176 See the Philippines, *Indigenous Peoples Rights Act 1997*, Section 3(c), definition of "*Sustainable Traditional Resource Rights*" which refers to "the rights of ICCs/IPs to sustainably use, manage, protect and conserve (a) land, air, water, and minerals; (b) plants, animals and other organisms; (c) collecting, fishing and hunting grounds; (d) sacred sites; and (e) other areas of economic, ceremonial and aesthetic value in accordance with their indigenous knowledge, beliefs, systems and practices".

Element

Consent to reside on land

The soil legislation should include:

- The procedure to establish rights to land.
- The method to obtain consent to reside on land and the period of residency.
- The conditions of development consent for sustainable use of soil.
- A description of allowable land uses, e.g., arable, pastoral, farm forestry uses.

Element

Rights and duties of owners

The rights and duties of land owners must be clearly spelt out in the legislation, including:[177]

- The definition of "owner" and categories of different types of owners.
- The respective duties to occupiers of the land.
- Provisions to prevent prejudice against occupiers.

Element

Transfer of land

The legislation should set out:

- The circumstances under which land ownership may be transferred.
- The conditions of land transfer.
- Any interim provisions for land transfer.
- The rights and responsibilities of landowners and occupiers during periods of land transfer.

3. Land management

Element

Right to participate in soil evaluation and soil planning

There should be special procedures to enable a land occupier or landowner to participate in soil evaluation and planning, soil rehabilitation and soil restoration programs, including:

- The administrative procedures for undertaking soil evaluation, soil planning, and soil rehabilitation and soil restoration.

---

177 See e.g., Waitangi Tribunal, 1991, *Ngai Tahu Report 1991* (3 vols), (Wai 27), Brooker and Friend, Wellington.

- The ecological soil standards to be used.
- The technical assistance provided by the soil authority.
- The availability of expert knowledge and technologies for small area agricultural land use.
- The specific role of occupiers and owners.

Element

Right to choose a farming system

There should be procedures in the legislation that enables occupiers and users to choose an appropriate farming system suitable for small area agriculture. Provisions can cover:

- The basic types and suitability of farming systems.
- The techniques to be employed to ensure the sustainable use of soil.
- The local and regional climatic constraints.
- The availability of markets.
- The benefits from establishing diversity in land use.[178]
- The flexibility and right to introduce new technologies.
- The administrative procedures to ensure security of tenure while using a particular farming system.

Element

Soil environmental management and soil husbandry

There should be procedures that enable occupiers and users to:

- Implement traditional land use techniques.
- Gain legal access to surface water and groundwater, and to maintain or improve water quality.
- Use a variety of soil husbandry techniques to improve the ecological integrity of soil.
- Use a variety of natural vegetation and crop husbandry techniques.
- Participate in soil education and knowledge building.
- Receive educational services from government and non-government sources.

178 See Stocking, M., 2002.

4. Land and soil agreements

Element

Formation and legal status of land occupation and soil use agreements

States can use special procedures to:

- Categorize the types of agreements that can be made between owners and occupiers.
- Set up agreements between government, owners and occupiers.
- Set out the conditions for soil and water use.
- Set out any special soil restoration measures.
- Amend, renew and expand agreements.
- Terminate agreements.
- Pay compensation to disadvantaged people who have been deprived access to land.

Element

Restoration of right of residence and use of soil

A State should include special provisions to:

- Set out conditions of right to reside on land.
- Set out conditions of reconstruction and maintenance.

5. Markets and farmer organizations

Element

Duty of government to find and secure markets

A State should include procedures in soil legislation to:

- Outline the responsibility of government to locate and secure markets for disadvantaged persons.[179]
- Enable effective coordination between government and representative groups of disadvantaged persons.

---

179 Special consideration should be given to the potential impacts of globalization on smallholder farming enterprises and local communities; see Reed, D., 2002, "Poverty and the Environment: Can Sustainable Development Survive Globalization?", *Natural Resources Forum*, 26:176; Concepcion and Nilo, 2001; see also, Kaul, I., I. Grunberg and M. Stern, Eds., 1999, *Global Public Goods – International Cooperation in the 21st Century*, UNDP, Oxford University Press.

Element

Provisions for farmer organizations

A State should include procedures in soil legislation to:

- Set out the role, functions and responsibilities of farmer organizations to disadvantaged people.
- Enable disadvantaged people to be properly represented in farmer organizations.
- Set out the role of the soil authority in farmer organizations.
- Enable effective communication with government.

6. Disputes and mediation

Element

Dispute resolution and courts

A State should include procedures in soil legislation to:[180]

- Outline the role and responsibility of a land claims court in relation to the special needs of disadvantaged people and the sustainable use of soil.
- Enable ready access of disadvantaged people to a court of law in relation to disputes over the sustainable use of soil.
- Set out procedures to enable disadvantaged people to obtain legal aid.

Element

Mediation

A State should include procedures in soil legislation to:[181]

- Establish a special mediation procedure for disadvantaged people.
- Ensure fair and equitable discussions, disclosures and submissions in relation to any dispute over the sustainable use of soil and disadvantaged people.
- Enable the appointment of a mediator conversant with special needs of disadvantaged people, particularly in relation to cultural and traditional matters and land use.

---

180 See Australia, New South Wales, *Land and Environment Court Act 1979;* see Part 3 "Jurisdiction of the Court"; *Protocol to the African Charter on Human and People's Rights on the Establishment of an African Court on Human and People's Rights*.

181 See Boulle, L., 1996, *Mediation: Principles, Process, Practice*, Butterworths, Sydney. "Mediation is a decision-making process in which the parties are assisted by a third party, the mediator; the mediator attempts to improve the process of decision-making and to assist the parties reach an outcome to which each of them can assent", p. 3.

Element

Offences

A State should include procedures in soil legislation to:

- Ensure that any offence alleged to have been carried out by a disadvantaged person is dealt with in a manner commensurate with the person's socio-economic, cultural or indigenous circumstances.
- Ensure that any penalty is commensurate with the person's socio-economic, cultural or indigenous circumstances.

7. Special regulations and guidelines

Element

Special regulations and guidelines

States should include procedures in soil legislation to:

- Prepare regulations for the sustainable use of soil that recognise the needs and requirements of disadvantaged people.
- Prepare guidelines in relation to any matter pertaining to the sustainable use of soil and the role, responsibilities, rights and needs of disadvantaged people.

VI. Glossary of terms for national soil legislation

"Agricultural land" means (a) land used for farming, agricultural, horticultural, viticulture, vegetable-growing, market gardening, pastoral, grazing, poultry farming, silvicultural, floricultural or piscicultural purposes, and (b) any other land declared to be farming lands for the purposes of soil legislation.[182]

"Biological diversity" means the variability among all sources, including, inter alia, terrestrial, marine, and other aquatic ecosystems and the ecological complexes of which they are part; this includes diversity within species, between species and of ecosystems.[183]

"Disadvantaged people" means a person or group of people engaged in, or who rely on agriculture and who, for various reasons, may be deprived of a reasonable standard of living, access to information, knowledge, health, education, opportunities, access to markets, and other services and benefits, by virtue of their socio-economic, cultural, ethnic or locational circumstances. (See Section V).

"Ecological integrity of soil" means preserving the wholeness of ecosystems, including the prevention of loss of wholeness, so as to stop the commencement of soil degradation, and to control existing soil degradation, and to protect and manage soil for its sustainable use.[184]

"Ecological soil standard" means a process for maintaining or improving the ecological integrity of soil.[185]

"Ecologically sustainable" means the sustained functioning of ecosystems by using appropriate ecological soil standards.[186]

"Existing or potentially threatening process" means a process applied to the soil or any other part of the ecosystem, which is or has the capability to threaten the ecological integrity of the soil.[187]

"Integrated resource management" is a process that promotes the coordinated development and management of water, land and related resources, in order to maximize the resultant economic and social welfare in an equitable manner without compromising the sustainability of vital ecosystems.[188]

---

182 Various definitions and meanings of "agricultural land", "agrarian land" exist – see Grossman and Brussaard, 1992.

183 UNEP, 1992, *Convention on Biological Diversity*, Nairobi.

184 Hannam with Boer, 2002, Section 2.

185 Hannam with Boer, 2002, Section 2.

186 Hannam with Boer, 2002, Section 2.

187 Hannam with Boer, 2002, Section 2.

188 Definition from Global Water Partnership, 2000, *Integrated Water Resources Management*, TAC Background Paper No. 4, Stockholm: Global Water Partnership, www.gwpcee.com/docs/TEC%204.pdf; and see *Supra*, Hannam 2004, for an example of the way this concept may be interpreted and applied in water and land management law reform.

"Land" means a delineable area of the earth's terrestrial surface, encompassing all attributes of the biosphere immediately above or below this surface, including those near the surface, the climate, the soil landscape, the ecosystems, the surface hydrology (including shallow lakes, rivers, marshes and swamps), the surface sedimentary layers and associated groundwater reserve, the animal populations, the human settlement pattern and physical results of past and present human activity (terracing, water storage or drainage structures, roads and buildings, etc.).[189]

"Prescribed activity" means an existing or potentially threatening process for which consent would be required before undertaking the activity.

"Soil" means the natural dynamic system of unconsolidated mineral and organic material at the earth's surface. It has been developed by physical, chemical and biological processes including the weathering of rock and the decay of vegetation. Soil is an integral part of the earth's ecosystems and is situated at the interface between the earth's surface and bedrock. It is subdivided into successive horizontal layers with specific physical, chemical and biological characteristics. From the standpoint of history of soil use, and from an ecological and environmental point of view, the concept of soil also embraces porous sedimentary rocks and other permeable materials together with the water that these contain and the reserves of underground water.[190]

"Soil advisory body" means an advisory committee constituted under national soil legislation.

"Soil association" means a soil mapping unit in which two or more soil taxonomic units occur together in a characteristic pattern, such as a toposequence. The units are combined because the scale of the map, or the purpose for which it is being made does not require delineation of individual soils. The soil association may be named according to the units present, the dominant unit, or be given a geographic name based on a locality where the soil association is well developed.[191]

"Soil biodiversity" means the biological diversity of soils, where areas of soil with common characteristics or qualities can be biologically classified and distinguished from other areas. Soil is an organism, has species characteristics (groups of soil with common characteristics or qualities), comprises genetic material and is biologically diverse. Soils can be grouped based on similarities of the soils within the group, and differences compared with other groups.[192]

"Soil conservation agreement" means an agreement entered into under soil legislation for the purpose of conserving the ecological integrity of soil.

"Soil conservation area" means the area of the soil environment subject to a soil conservation agreement.

"Soil conservation" is any technical or non-technical process applied to the soil, to ensure that soil, together with all other aspects of the ecosystem, is conserved.

---

189 FAO, 1995, *Planning for Sustained Use of Land Resources: Towards a New Approach*, Rome, FAO.

190 See Council of Europe 1990, *European Conservation Strategy*, Recommendations for the 6th European Ministerial Conference on the Environment, Strasbourg, Council of Europe.

191 Houghton, P.D., and P.E.V. Charman, 1986, *Glossary of Terms Used in Soil Conservation*, Soil Conservation Service of NSW, Australian Standing Committee on Soil Conservation.

192 Hannam with Boer, 2002, Section 2.

"Soil degradation" includes aspects of physical, chemical and/or biological deterioration. Examples are loss of organic matter, decline in soil fertility, decline in structural condition, soil erosion, adverse changes in salinity, acidity or alkalinity and the effects of toxic chemicals, pollutants or excessive flooding.

"Soil ecological community" is a generic term which means an area of land which has been identified by mapping, and according to specified soil ecological criteria, that interacts as an identifiable functional or spatial unit. It is synonymous with a "soil landscape". Other terms that may also be used interchangeably with the concept of a "soil ecological community", include "soil quality", "soil type", "soil ecosystems", "soil resources".[193]

"Soil environment" is the natural dynamic system of unconsolidated mineral and organic material at the earth's surface, which interacts with the living community of earth and the natural, human-made and social surroundings of that community.

"Soil environmental impact assessment" means a report evaluating the likely impact of an activity on the ecological integrity of soil.

"Soil functions" means the different functions of soils: the habitat function, the regulation function, the utilisation function and the cultural function.

"Soil landscape" means an area of land that has recognisable and specifiable topography that is capable of being presented on maps and of being described by concise statements. Thus a soil landscape has a characteristic landform with one or more soil taxonomic units occurring in a defined way. It is often associated with the physiographic features of the landscape and is similar to a soil association, but in a soil landscape the landform pattern is specifically described. The soil landscape may be named according to the soil taxonomic units present, the dominant unit, or be given a geographic name based on a locality where it is well developed.[194]

"Soil quality" means the capacity of a specific type of soil to function, within natural or fabricated ecosystems or land use boundaries, to sustain plant and animal productivity, maintain or enhance water and air quality and support human health and habitation.[195]

"State soil strategy" means the strategy prepared under national soil legislation to set out how the objectives of soil legislation will be achieved.

"Sustainable use of soil" means the use of soils in a manner that preserves the balance between the processes of soil formation and soil degradation, while maintaining the ecological functions and needs of soil. In this context, "the use of soil" means 'the role of soil in the conservation of biodiversity and the maintenance of human life'.[196]

---

193 See Australia, *Environment Protection and Biodiversity Conservation Act 1999*, Chapter 5 "Conservation of Biodiversity".

194 Houghton, P.D. and P.E.V. Charman, 1986, p. 118.

195 Kerlen, D.L., J.W. Mausbach, J.W. Doran, R.G. Cline, R.F. Harris, G.E. Schuman, 1995, Soil Quality: A concept, definition, and framework for evaluation, *Soil Science Society of America Journal*, 61, 4–10.

196 Hannam with Boer, 2002, Section 2.

"Works" means any soil conservation technique necessary for the conservation of soil or the mitigation of soil degradation and any operations incidental thereto: Any "work" should benefit the ecological integrity of soil.

VII. Application of multilateral and regional environmental law instruments and strategies

The following multilateral instruments, declarations, agreements and other strategic materials can be consulted as part of the approach to reform or develop new legislation or policy on sustainable soil.[197]

A. International instruments

- 1971 Convention on Wetlands of International Importance Especially as Waterfowl Habitat[198]
- 1972 Convention for the Protection of the World Cultural and Natural Heritage[199]
- 1972 Convention on the Prevention of Marine Pollution by Dumping of Waste and other Matter[200]
- 1973 Convention on International Trade in Endangered Species of Wild Fauna and Flora[201]
- 1982 United Nations Convention on the Law of the Sea[202]
- 1985 Vienna Convention for the Protection of the Ozone Layer[203]
- 1989 ILO Convention (No. 169) concerning Indigenous and Tribal Peoples in Independent Countries[204]

---

197 Refer to expert legal database for detailed information on relevant instruments; see ECOLEX (www.ecolex.org), an information service on environmental law, operated jointly by FAO, IUCN and UNEP. ECOLEX combines the environmental law information holdings of FAO, IUCN and UNEP, for the disposal of users world-wide, in an easily accessible service. The ECOLEX database includes information on treaties, international soft-law and other non-binding policy and technical guidance documents, national legislation, judicial decisions, and law and policy literature. Users have direct access to the abstracts and indexing information about each document, as well as to the full text of most of the information provided.

198 Place of adoption: Ramsar; date of adoption: 2 February 1971; available in: 996 UNTS 243.

199 Place of adoption: Paris; date of adoption: 16 November 1972; available in: 1037 UNTS 151.

200 Entry into force: 30 August 1975; available in: 1046 UNTS 120.

201 Place of adoption: Washington, D.C.; date of adoption: 3 March 1973; entry into force: 1 July 1975; available in: 983 UNTS 243.

202 Place of adoption: Montego Bay; date of adoption: 10 December 1982; BGBl. 1994 II 1798; available in: EMuT 982:92.

203 Place of adoption: Vienna; date of adoption: 22 March 1985; available in: 1513 UNTS 324, EMuT 985:22.

204 Adopted on 27 June 1989 by the General Conference of the International Labour Organisation at its seventy-sixth session; entry into force: 5 September 1991; available in: 1650 UNTS 351.

- Basel Convention on the Control of Transboundary Movements of Hazardous Wastes and their Disposal[205]
- 1992 Convention on Biological Diversity[206]
- 1992 United Nations Framework Convention on Climate Change[207]
- 1992 Convention on the Protection and Use of Transboundary Watercourses and International Lakes[208]
- 1995 United Nations Convention to Combat Desertification in Countries Experiencing Serious Drought and/or Desertification, Particularly Africa[209]
- 1987 Montreal Protocol on Substances that Deplete the Ozone Layer[210]
- 1997 Kyoto Protocol to the United Nations Framework Convention on Climate Change[211]
- 1998 Convention on the Protection of the Environment through Criminal Law[212]
- 1999 Protocol on Water and Health to the 1992 Convention on the Protection and Use of Transboundary Watercourses and International Lakes[213]

International Declarations

- 1948 Universal Declaration of Human Rights[214]
- 1972 (Stockholm) Declaration of the United Nations Conference on the Human Environment[215]
- 1992 Rio Declaration on Environment and Development[216]

---

205 Place of adoption: Basel; date of adoption: 22 March 1989; entry into force: 5 May 1992; available in: 1821 UNTS 369, EMuT 989:22.

206 Place of adoption: Rio de Janeiro; date of adoption: 5 June 1992; available in: 1760 UNTS 142.

207 Place of adoption: New York; date of adoption: 9 May 1992; entry into force: 21 March 1994; available in: 1771 UNTS 164, EMuT 992:35.

208 Place of adoption: Helsinki; date of adoption: 17 March 1992; entry into force: 10 June 1996; available in: 1936 UNTS 269, EMuT 992:20.

209 Place of adoption: Paris; date of adoption: 17 June 1994; entry into force: 26 December 1996; available in: 1954 UNTS 107, EMuT 994:76.

210 Place of adoption: Montreal; date of adoption: 16 September 1987; available in: 1522 UNTS 28, EMuT 985:22/A.

211 Place of adoption: Kyoto; date of adoption: 11 December 1997; available in: 1971 UNTS 164, EMuT 992:35/A.

212 Place of adoption: Strasbourg; date of adoption: 4 November 1998; Council of Europe, COE No. 172; available in: EMuT 998:82.

213 Place of adoption: London; date of adoption: 17 June 1999; available in: EMuT 992:20/A.

214 Adopted and proclaimed by General Assembly resolution 217 A (III), 10 December 1948.

215 Stockholm, 16 June, printed in 11 ILM (1972) 1416. "International Environmental Soft Law", W.E. Burhenne, (Ed.), Marlene Jahnke, ICEL, Martinus Nijhoff Publishers, Dordrecht, Netherlands, 2002, (hereinafter "SL"), 972–4505.

216 United Nations Conference on Environment and Development (UNCED), United Nations Document, A/CONF.151/5/Rev. 1, 1992, Preamble printed in 31 ILM (1992), 874, SL 992:4405.

- 1995 Washington Declaration on Protection of the Marine Environment from Land-Based Activities[217]

Other strategies

- 1982 World Charter for Nature[218]
- 1994 International Tropical Timber Agreement[219]
- 1992 Non-Legally Binding Authoritative Statement of Principles for a Global Consensus on the Management, Conservation and Sustainable Development of all Types of Forests[220]
- The Dublin Statement on Water and Sustainable Development[221]
- 1992 Agenda 21[222]
- 2004 IUCN Draft International Covenant on Environment and Development[223]
- 2002 Johannesburg Declaration on Sustainable Development[224]
- 2002 World Summit on Sustainable Development Plan of Implementation[225]

B. Regional instruments

- 1974 Convention Establishing a Permanent Inter-State Drought Control Committee for the Sahel[226]

---

217 The representatives of Governments and the European Commission participating in the Conference held in Washington from 23 October to 3 November 1995; www.unep.org/unep/gpa/pol2b12.htm, "International Protection of the Environment: Conservation in Sustainable Development" 2004, Wolfgang E. Burhenne, Nicholas A. Robinson (eds), Oceana Publications Inc., Dobbs Ferry, New York (hereinafter "BuRo"), 01-11-95/2.

218 United Nations General Assembly Resolution 37/7, 1982, printed in 22 ILM (1983), 455, available in: SL 982:8005.

219 Place of adoption: Geneva; date of adoption: 18 November 1983; entry into force: 1 January 1997; available in: EMuT 994:07.

220 *Non-Legally Binding Authoritative Statement of Principles for Global Consensus on the Management, Conservation and Sustainable Development of All Types of Forests*, adopted at UNCED 1992; see Tarasofsky, R.G., 1995, *The International Forests Regime, Legal and Policy Issues*. IUCN, The World Conservation Union, World Wide Fund for Nature, p. 20-21; available in: SL 992:4435.

221 International Conference on Water and Environment (UN, Dublin): set out the four principles of water resource management that came to be known as the Dublin Principles; see www.wmo.ch/web/homs/documents/english/icwedece.html, The Dublin Statement On Water And Sustainable Development; and M. Solanes and F. Gonzalez-Villarreal, 1999, *The Dublin Principles for Water as Reflected in a Comparative Assessment of Institutional and Legal Arrangements for Integrated Water Resources Management*, TAC Background paper No 3, Global Water Partnership/Swedish International Development Cooperation Agency S105-25 Stockholm, Sweden.

222 United Nations Conference on Environment and Development (UNCED), United Nations Document, A/CONF.151/6/Rev. 1, 1992, printed in 31 ILM (1992), 881.

223 *Supra*, Environmental Policy and Law Paper (EPLP) No. 31 Rev 2, 3rd edition, IUCN, Cambridge, 2004.

224 *Supra*, WSSD, 2002; available in: BuRo: 20-08-2002/1.

225 *Supra*, WSSD, 2002; available in: SL 2002:7805.

226 Place of adoption: Ouagadougou; date of adoption: 12 September 1973; available in: EMuT 973:67.

- 1976 Convention on Conservation of Nature in the South Pacific[227]
- 1976 Convention for the Protection of the Mediterranean Sea against Pollution[228]
- 1982 Protocol concerning Mediterranean Specially Protected Areas[229]
- 1983 Benelux Convention on Nature Conservation and Landscape Protection[230]
- 1983 Protocol for the Protection of South-East Pacific against Pollution from Land-Based Sources[231]
- 1985 Convention for the Protection, Management and Development of the Marine and Coastal Environment of the Eastern African Region[232]
- 1990 Convention for the Protection of Natural Resources and Environment of the South Pacific Region[233]
- 1991 Convention on Environmental Impact Assessment in a Transboundary Context[234]
- 1991 Convention on the Protection of the Alps (Alpine Convention)[235]
- 1992 Convention for the Conservation of the Biodiversity and Protection of Wilderness Areas in Central America[236]
- Convention for the Management and Conservation of Natural Forest Ecosystems and the Development of Forest Plantations[237]
- 1994 Protocol for the Implementation of the Alpine Convention in the Field of Mountain Agriculture[238]

227 Place of adoption: Apia; date of adoption: 12 June 1976; entry into force: 28 June 1990; available in: EMuT 976:45.

228 Place of adoption: Barcelona; date of adoption: 16 February 1976; entry into force: 12 February 1978; available in: EMuT 976:13.

229 Place of adoption: Geneva; date of adoption: 3 April 1982; entry into force: 23 March 1986; available in: EMuT 976:13/D.

230 Place of adoption: Bruxelles; date of adoption: 8 June 1982; entry into force: 1 October 1983; available in: EMuT 982:43.

231 Place of adoption: Quito; date of adoption: 22 July 1983; entry into force: 23 September 1986; available in: EMuT 981:84/A.

232 Place of adoption: Nairobi; date of adoption: 21 June 1985; entry into force: 30 May 1996; available in: EMuT 985:46.

233 Place of adoption: Nouméa; date of adoption: 24 November 1986; available in: EMuT 986:87.

234 Place of adoption: Espoo; date of adoption: 25 February 1991; entry into force: 10 September 1997; available in: 1989 UNTS 309, EMuT 991:15.

235 Place of adoption: Salzburg; date of adoption: 7 November 1991; entry into force: 6 March 1995; available in: EMuT 991:83.

236 Place of adoption: Managua; date of adoption: 5 June 1992; available in: EMuT 992:43.

237 Place of adoption: Guatemala City; date of adoption: 29 October 1993; entry into force: 15 October 1999; available in: EMuT 993:80.

238 Place of adoption: Chambery; date of adoption: 20 December 1994; entry into force: 18 December 2002; available in: EMuT 991:83/C.

- 1994 Protocol for the Implementation of the Alpine Convention in the Field of Nature Protection and Landscape Conservation[239]
- 1995 Protocol on Shared Watercourse Systems in the Southern African Development Community (SADC) Region[240]
- 1996 Protocol for the Implementation of the Alpine Convention in the field of Mountain Forests[241]
- 1998 Convention on Access to Information, Public Participation in Decision-Making and Access to Justice in Environmental Matters[242]
- 1998 The Protocol for the Implementation of the Alpine Convention in the Field of Soil Protection[243]
- 1999 Protocol Concerning Specially Protected Areas and Biological Diversity in the Mediterranean[244]
- 2000 European Landscape Convention[245]
- 2000 African Convention on the Conservation of Nature and Natural Resources[246]
- 2000 Revised Protocol on Shared Watercourses in the Southern Africa Development Community (SADC)[247]
- 2000 Protocol for the Implementation of the Alpine Convention Concerning Dispute Settlement[248]
- 2003 Protocol on Strategic Environmental Assessment to the Convention on Environmental Impact Assessment in a Transboundary Context[249]

---

239 Place of adoption: Chambery; date of adoption: 20 December 1994; entry into force: 18 December 2002; available in: EMuT 991:83/D.

240 Place of adoption: Johannesburg; date of adoption: 28 August 1995; entry into force: 29 September 1998; available in: EMuT 992:62/A.

241 Place of adoption: Brdo; date of adoption: 27 February 1996; entry into force: 18 December 2002; available in: EMuT 991:83/E.

242 Place of adoption: Aarhus; date of adoption: 25 June 1998; entry into force: 30 October 2001; available in: 2161 UNTS 450, EMuT 998:48.

243 Place of adoption: Bled; date of adoption: 16 October 1998; entry into force: 18 December 2002; available in: EMuT 991:83/F.

244 Place of adoption: Barcelona; date of adoption: 10 June 1995; Official Journal of the European Communities (OJEC), L 322, 14/12/1999, pp. 3–17.

245 Place of adoption: Florence; date of adoption: 20 October 2000; available in: EMuT 2000:78.

246 Place of adoption: Maputo; date of adoption: 11 July 2003; available in EMuT 2003:52.

247 Place of adoption: Windhoek; date of adoption: 7 August 2000; available in: EMuT 992:62/G.

248 Place of adoption: Lausanne; date of adoption: 31 October 2000; entry into force: 18 December 2002; available in: EMuT 991:83/J.

249 Place of adoption: Kiev; date of adoption: 21 May 2003; available in: UN Doc. ECE/MP.EIA/2003/2, EMuT 991:15/B.

Agreements

- 1971 Agreement for the Establishment of the Arab Centre for the Studies of Dry and Barren Land
- 1976 Agreement concerning the Protection of the Waters of the Mediterranean Shores[250]
- 1983 Agreement for the Establishment of a Regional Centre on Agrarian Reform and Rural Development for the Near East[251]
- 1985 ASEAN Agreement on the Conservation of Nature and Natural Resources[252]
- 1995 Agreement on the Cooperation for the Sustainable Development of the Mekong River Basin[253]

Other strategies

- 1989 The Langkawi Declaration on the Environment[254]
- 1998 Memorandum of Understanding between the Republic of Kenya and the United Republic of Tanzania and Republic of Uganda for Cooperation on Environment Management[255]
- 1994 The East Asian Seas Action Plan[256]

250 Place of adoption: Monaco; date of adoption: 10 May 1976; entry into force: 1 January 1981; available in: EMuT 976:36.

251 Place of adoption: Rome; date of adoption: 28 September 1983; entry into force: 30 December 1987.

252 Place of adoption: Kuala Lumpur; date of adoption: 9 July 1985; available in: EMuT 985:51.

253 Place of adoption: Chiang Rai; date of adoption: 5 April 1995; entry into force: 5 April 1995; available in: 206 UNTS 4, EMuT 995:26.

254 Signed on October 21st, 1989 in conjunction with the Commonwealth Head of Government Meeting (CHOGM) on 18–24 October 1989 in Langkawi, Malaysia, see www.jas.sains.my/jas/Masm/langkawideclaration.htm

255 Place of adoption: Nairobi; date of adoption: 22 October 1998; available in: EMuT 998:79.

256 Adopted in 1981; Secretariat: Regional coordinating unit for the East Asian seas action plan, UNEP, 10th Floor, United Nations Building, Rajdamnern Avenue, Bangkok 10200, Thailand; see www.unep.org/water/regseas/easian.htm